The Visit

Also by Sharon Doubiago

memoir
My Father's Love, Volume I: Portrait of the Poet as a Young Girl
*My Father's Love, Volume II: The Legacy, Portrait of the Poet as a
        Woman*

poetry
Chinatown
Hymn to the Cosmic Clothesline
Visions of a Daughter of Albion
Hard Country
Oedipus Drowned
Psyche Drives the Coast
South America Mi Hija
The Husband Arcane.   The Arcane of O
Body and Soul
Greatest Hits
Love on the Streets

stories
The Book of Seeing With One's Own Eyes
El Niño

editor
*Wood, Water, Air and Fire, The Anthology of Mendocino Women
        Poets* with Devreaux Baker and Susan Maeder
The Dalmo'ma Anthologies and Empty Bowl Press with Michael
Daley and the Ohode Collective, 1980-1987.
Western Edge: 33 Poets, with Bill Bradd and Duane BigEagle

The Visit

A Poem

by

Sharon Doubiago

Wild Ocean Press
San Francisco

Lines quoted from *Hard Country,* West End Press, 1982, 1999; *The Book of Seeing With One's Own Eyes*, Graywolf, 1988; *Psyche Drives The Coast*, Empty Bowl, 1990; *South America Mi Hija,* University of Pittsburgh, 1992; *The Husband Arcane.   The Arcane of O,* Gorda Plate Press, 1996; *Body and Soul,* Cedar Hill Publications, 2000; *Love on the Streets, Selected and New Poems*, University of Pittsburgh, 2008; *My Father's Love, Volumes I and II,* Wild Ocean Press, 2009, 2011.

Cover Photo Credits: foreground image, R.D. Deines, *New Settler Interview* by permission; background image, Charles Gentile/ Library and Archives Canada/C-088931 (copyright expired).

Back cover portrait of Sharon Doubiago: Photograph, Deidre Lamb, All Rights Reserved; used by permission of Kelley House Museum, Mendocino, California.

Cover design by Theresa Whitehill, Colored Horse Studios
http://coloredhorse.com/

ISBN: 978-1-941137-04-8

Printed in the United States of America

First edition, first printing

Distributed by Small Press Distribution, Inc., Berkeley, CA
http://www.spdbooks.org

Wild Ocean Press
San Francisco, CA 94133
www.wildoceanpress.com

for Kha-che-chee

and

all victims of sexual violations

Table of Contents

Preface: I Am My Brother's Keeper

Jack Retasket is a Native American/Canadian Shuswap-Lillooet (Statlmx) survivor of Kamloops Indian Residential School where he was imprisoned at the age of five—legally separated from this twin sister, his mother and father, ten other brothers and sisters, home and tribe. At seven he was raped by his Oblate, Brother Shirley; his account of that rape is at the center of this poem. At thirteen he ran away from Kamloops—across the U.S. border to Oroville, Washington to his family who had fled there to work as apple pickers in order to escape the mandatory placing of their younger children into Kamloops; the parents themselves had been incarcerated there as children. In 2004 at the age of 54, Jack Retasket was arrested and convicted of sexual violation of a female child under twelve, his girlfriend's daughter seven years previously, and sentenced to fifteen years in Oregon's Two Rivers Correctional Institution. "The Visit" is an investigative poem in the Ed Sanders' tradition, a protest poem, and a love poem.

I was completing the first draft of *My Father's Love*, the memoir of my father's sexual violation of me from infancy to twelve, when Jack was arrested. One month after his arrest, Neil Goldschmidt, the popular ex-Governor of Oregon confessed to a similar crime but the statute of limitations meant he could not be arrested. Six months later Jack was found guilty in Newport Oregon. "The Visit" tells Jack's full story as I know it and he has allowed me, and invokes the contrite Goldschmidt for his help, *"that you work to free him/that you find self-forgiveness in this act of atonement."* [1]

In the beginning I believed Jack, that he is innocent. Then through the slowly evolving meditation, our correspondence, my attempted poem here and my own background, I came to consider that he is possibly guilty. How do I write that and maintain my fidelity to both him and to my vision? What is my responsibility? To his victim? What is my responsibility to society, to myself? Whatever, the unequal treatment, legal and social, of these two men, Goldschmidt and Retasket, is blatant. [2]

The earliest version of "The Visit" was three pages, completed in 2006, soon after my first prison visit to Jack. I read it in a reading I gave at the San Francisco/North Beach Library. A woman poet friend, who I respect and love, a grieving widow who is a kind of lay nun for the Catholic Church here in San Francisco, said something like "all this stuff is just people out to destroy the Catholic Church." That pretty much stopped me then: I had failed in the task of my poem. But then came the 2011 revelations of Elizabeth Lynn Dunham on her deathbed at forty-nine, the once thirteen year old daughter of Governor Goldschmidt's campaign manager, and still more of Goldschmidt's contrite disclosures. In the long process of writing *My Father's Love,* I'd gained the strength to withstand the world's denial and condemnation (including of my family and friends), but these ongoing developments with Jack Retasket and Neil Goldschmidt were devastating. The last time I saw my beautiful San Francisco Catholic friend, in 2013, she told me that she was sexually violated by her older brother. Then she more or less disappeared from my life again.

In the beginning I had the intent of requesting Neil Goldschmidt's support, and so in the poem I named Jack by his names, places and stories, ways that the crime of which he is accused and convicted could be tracked. Now, ten years later, the poem has a different feel, a different intent, perhaps. Jack is beginning to anticipate his release in four years, of returning to his Canadian Reservation home, and/or of enrolling/being employed in his sisters' Native programs at Northwest Indian College—formerly Lummi Community College—of starting a new life (at age 68). And so a new issue: should I disguise him now? His articulate, beautiful letters fill many boxes; I've visited him twice (only twice, having returned from my long residency in Washington and Oregon to California). Though I personally dislike the telephone I accept most of his calls. He's been suicidal at least twice since his sentencing in 2004, and is physically handicapped from the first attempt in Lincoln County Jail when the new Measure 11 guilty verdict came in. Loyal that I've been and am, I do fear that revealing that I consider him possibly guilty could cause him once again to try and off himself. I've given him the choice of disguises; he insists that I "go for it." (But the prison censors won't allow him to read sections #3, 4, and 5 here, though most are his own words which he wrote and sent out from there.) I pray he has found the inner strength and political and inspirational wisdom to stand by his insistence, and realizes the deep healing and spiritual quest possible for all of us in such work.

The Visit

Few have understood my fidelity and unwavering love for my father which I learned through prayer and my childhood church, Trinity Bible Church up on the corner of Industrial and Main, in Hollydale, California. The soul-deep example and spiritual lesson of Jesus saved my sanity. (I do not refute that now, though—and I must state this—I disavow the Christian church.) Jesus taught me to Love and to Forgive and to know a kind of Negative Capability, John Keats' complexity of thought and possibility. I never hated my father, I hated what he did to me. *"Forgive them Father, they know not what they do."* Black and white thinking, as my father himself lectured (though trying to beat me down) is war mentality; truth and genuine resolutions are found in deeper approaches.

My knowledge of the State's perpetuation of the problem and suffering is not altered from what I knew at seven. I do not regret the protection of my father then and I would repeat it today. I do regret my family's and society's vast psychosis, the inability to address what has been labeled as humanity's oldest sin. I think I finally comprehend the depth of my father's violation of me—and of all men who violate children.

I have the deep sense that male sexual violations, especially of their daughters and sons and other young ones, is largely a cultural/patriarchal phenomenon not wholly or solely natural to the male, as is fiercely maintained. Male sexual violations are about the male role, learned. The male role is psychological, manipulative. Prescribed, not organic. Habitual: once learned, nearly irreversible. If there are cultural studies of human sexual violations outside the reported ones—Christian, Judaic, Buddhist. Hindu, Moslem, et al, all based on the notion of male gender superiority—I have not found them.

In our patriarchy the boy, helpless and in love with his mother, grows up to find his manhood in overpowering women. Especially his wives (and daughters and sons that come from her body). This is one of our most simple and clear reversals, but which, along with rape, we seem unable to examine. Somewhere I have a poem about human fecal and urinary control. Universally, the very young human gains control of this profound physiological phenomenon. We could, and must, do the same, sexually.

Our sexual perversities are a bad shadow of patriarchy. There are in fact other cultures through time which are not of the murderous, sexually crazed mania that we are. But to pursue study of such is problematic because the published journalists, writers, memoirists, scholars, religious leaders, poets and thinkers on other cultures are profoundly rooted in our own.

The Cherokee, for instance, of which I am part, is matriarchal (or was); the male is the "father" figure for his sisters' children, not of his own, this in recognition of the psychotic imbalance of power that patriarchy would give him. Divorce is simply the wife putting his stuff outside their dwelling; he returns to his mother and sisters' homes.

Once I had a love who, leaving the Catholic seminary in his early twenties where he had been sexually violated from early teens, spent two years in the so-called Combat Zone of Boston, the prostitution neighborhood, to overcome his attraction to young boy students, to not repeat what had been done to him—and done to Jack in Kamloops Indian Residential School. (Shockingly, my otherwise fine, still usable Webster's New World 1984 Dictionary defines rape as *"the crime of sexual intercourse with a woman or girl forcibly and without her consent."* There has been little accounting of forcible adult male sex with boys, a blatant bias and tragic inaccuracy of patriarchal scholarship. I've actually heard men exclaim that this is not homosexuality!)

One of my earliest readings of the work that became my father memoir was in Ukiah, California, 2000, where through the years I've been an honored poet and writer. Afterwards, one man asked, genuinely, it seemed, "Do you ever deal with why?" I continued to think on that question a long time, actually it sort of haunted me. He meant that I was irresistible to my father. Thus the poem here, "Irresistible," long in the making. (Again, we learn urinary and fecal control of our otherwise irresistible physical urges and needs.) "Irresistible" sex is a much promoted, celebrated patriarchal myth.

A Mendocino male poet friend shared with me, in innocence, or so it seemed, his long meditation on whether he should have sex with his daughter, that, conceivably, it was his paternal duty! I had heard this debate all my life, starting with my beloved Gae at seven, who was also being sexed by her father, her parents being early members of the Sexual Freedom League which advocated such sex. In the end he assured me that he decided he shouldn't (probably in response to the active feminism there and my not responding to his sharing) but again, outrageously, his pondering that it was his responsibility seemed genuine. I think here of the two contemporary French philosophers, Jacques Derrida and Michael Foucault who advocated sex with children, in vast evil blindness to what constitutes the human soul.

As an Oglala Miniconjou Lakota Sioux,[3] what was Crazy Horse's sexuality? What were his sexual fantasies after age thirteen when he found the body of his secret love, the sister of Long Spear at the Sand Creek Massacre? Her pudendum was scalped, a practice not uncommon among the US Army in the western Indian wars; soldiers wore scalped Native vulvas on their caps.

> *"and the boy Crazy Horse sees with great lightning spears*
> *that are brighter than the sun, as thunders shake the earth,*
> *these dead ones with their faces open to the storm*
> *are his people*
>
> *fetuses lying outside their mothers'*
> *knifed-opened bellies*
>
> *and the blue-painted dress*
> *when he pulls it down from her face*
> *is the young sister of Long Spear*
> *her wide sleeves like flying wings pulled up*
> *and she is scalped in a bad place"* [4]

All my life I've pondered Native American cultures (and other non-western ones around the world), mainly the matriarchal ones, as holding possible solutions to our sexual pathologies—different psychologies, sexualities, values, social customs, organization, spirituality and love. I've developed methods of writing memoir (including memoir poems), methods and aesthetics of remembering and writing that are contrary to many contemporary memoir aesthetics and practices (mainly that memory is fallible, unreliable; that making things up is the Creative, the Poetic). Because I was always labeled a liar by my family terrified that I would tell, verifiable facts are important to me. My need not to make a mistake or tell an untruth, not to consciously fictionalize or fabricate, is immense, is spiritual. (But of course, mistakes are not entirely avoidable.)

In my life-long, prayed-for story my father confesses his mistake and terrible violation of me, which in fact he did do four months before his death (*My Father's Love*, Volume II, Chapter 17)—though inadequate to the life-long violation, psychic as much as physical, that he imposed on me and all the family. In my dream he is confessing because he knows the damage he did to me, to all of us, and to himself. In his confession I am meeting him. I am not falling to that other pole, I am not sadomasochistic. I am his keeper.

Sharon Doubiago
January 23, 2015
Mendocino, California

*

The Visit

Invocation

*"If we could read the secret history of our enemies, we should find in each man's life sorrow
and suffering enough to disarm all hostility."* Henry Wadsworth Longfellow

"I wish my adopted children to achieve amnesia….I want them to be well." Michael Dorris[8]

"I ovulate against us." Sharon Doubiago, *The Husband Arcane.*   *The Arcane of O* [9]

Dear Neil Goldschmidt,[10]
Kha-che-chee, Canadian American First Nation
Native: Shuswap and Lillooet
productive resident of Newport Oregon for thirty years
was arrested April 6, 2004 exactly one month
before you confessed, May 6, 2004

to the same crime, though yours
is perhaps more serious and he maintains
he is innocent.

But because you are the former mayor of Portland,
the former governor of Oregon, "Oregon's most
successful and charismatic leader," the web site still says,
"the most powerful political figure of the second half of the century"

you suffer only humiliation, guilt and career
not the loss of the riches you amassed from your privileged positions
while Kha-che-chee is put away for basically the rest of his life.

This is classism, Neil Goldschmidt, blatant
racism. And so I'm addressing my poem to you.
I'm asking you to help find justice, to find amnesty
for "Jack Retasket."

Amnesty is forgiveness, not forgetting. Not
amnesia. This poem
seeks amnesty, full memory.
"First the truth, then reconciliation." This poem
seeks you
to make amends
from the position of your privilege

that you work to free him
that you find self-forgiveness in this act of atonement

that Kha-che-chee find justice
and healing, that all victims
of abuse and molestation
find justice and healing

*"Beginning in 1975, while I was mayor, I had an affair with a high school student
for nearly a year. In 1994, I funded a conservatorship in her behalf, believing
I was partly responsible for her difficulties coping with her life.*

*For almost thirty years, I have lived with enormous guilt and shame
about this relationship. I have also been afraid that it would be exposed
to my family, friends and the public whose respect I have sought to earn.*

*How can such behavior be erased when the damage to others and to myself lives on?
I have sat in my place of worship each year at Yom Kippur, the day of atonement
in my religious tradition, reading in silence, searching for personal peace.
And I have found that the answer to that question is
it cannot be erased.*

*The pain and damage that I have caused have been with me constantly.
I have known all along that my private apologies and actions, deep and true
though they were, would never be enough. I apologize now, publicly and completely.*

*I am truly sorry for allowing the relationship to happen at all, with someone too young
to be responsible or accountable for her actions; for failing my first wife; and for betraying
the trust of family, friends and all those who put their trust in me.*

*In my life I have been blessed with a loving and supportive family, wonderful children
and grandchildren, and a wife who helped me confront this issue.*

*With all sincerity, I pray that God will accept my contrition and protect my family
from the pain that a life led poorly in part may bring to their homes. May a forgiving God
mend my broken heart and those I have broken. And may Oregonians accept this apology,
even if they cannot forgive my actions."*[11,12]

Elizabeth Lynn Dunham was born May 12, 1961
and died January 16, 2011. Only then, with her death, do we learn
her name, age and story

There followed uproar that you called your sexual abuse
of a thirteen year old girl
"an affair"

that she was thirteen, not fourteen as you later claimed
in junior high, not high school

That you kept it up for four years, not "for nearly a year"[13]
        actually, until she was twenty-seven, but once she was seventeen
        it was no longer a criminal act.
That in Oregon sex with a person under seventeen is rape
that you didn't confess
until you were safe behind the statute of limitations
and the Willamette Week was going to press with its findings[14]
that her mother was your close friend and campaign worker
that the January of her eighth grade year, at her mother's birthday party,
a house full of adults, '*Neil asked me*

> *if I wanted to play ping pong.*
> *We went down into the basement, and then he said, 'Oh*
> *do you want to come give me a hug?'*
> *It turned into much more than a hug. It turned into oral sex.*
> *I was afraid. I was a virgin. I'd never even kissed a boy. Far*
> *from it.* "[15]

That regularly through those years of her childhood
and your public service to us
you left your house, your wife, your children
to go the three blocks to her house

Driving by, home from the office, you had a code with the lights
so she would know whether you were coming in or not.
You never drove yourself, you always had
a trusted driver. Everyone on your staff
knew of Elizabeth, except, supposedly
her mother

That with you as Portland's "beloved mayor"
as "Oregon's most charismatic Governor," Elizabeth
went crazy, went to booze, drugs, the street, years circling

your downtown Mayor's Office, your governor's mansion in Salem, our
American witch returned from the Dead, circling
those who knew and were subsequently enriched
and empowered in Oregon politics and business

I accept your apology, Neil Goldschmidt
        as I accept Kha-che-chee's plea of innocence
        as I accepted my father's confession

                "I never forgot for a single day what I did to you
                I'm sorry Lu if I hurt you."
                But he wasn't sorry enough
                to stop himself from repeating
                the same molestation of my brother's daughter.

I accept that you do comprehend the harm
you have caused, the violations
you committed

the harm that continues
the pain Elizabeth Lynn Dunham suffered onto early death
the guilt you suffer, the pain we all
suffer

that you seek a path for us all
this crime most common, this crime most denied

Some say you should be in prison.
I say no one, especially Kha-che-chee, innocent or not
should be in prison. Prison
is sadomasochism, the reinforcement of our national psychic pattern, our
psycho ways, our sick sex and religion of conquest. The only justice
the only healing, is in full memory: that we know
what we did, that we know
what was done to us

                that we know of Kha-che-chee's kidnapping at five by
                        the State and Church
                from his mother and father, from his brothers and sisters,
                from his twin sister

      that we know the loss of his language, his tribe, his culture.
      The loss of his name, of his being renamed Jack
      by the State and Church

      that we know of his rape at seven by the Oblate
      of Kamloops Indian Residential school

      that we know the theft of himself from himself
      that we know the mental illness we create
      that we cause the soul loss
      that becomes sexual obsession

Domination and submission is not democracy, Governor.
Only justice can stop a curse. Amnesty
is remembering. This poem seeks
full memory. We, the only nation
without a Truth and Reconciliation Commission

Your confession is the first step. You could do more.
You could understand
the curse. You could fight
to free Kha-che-chee, all the victims
of untold, immeasurable wrongs.

This plea, this poem, this petition, this
prayer to you. This Yom Kippur
to all

This poem, this United States' Truth
and Reconciliation Commission

You could free
our love, our Crazy Horse, our Leonard Peltier
You could save Kha-che-chee

*

*"When I say I was raped at eight will people understand
what I truly mean? The ongoing complications 30 years after
an adult seducer permanently interfered with my sexual development?
I wasn't physically forced or brutally violated. In fact—and this
was what I was most profoundly ashamed of—my penis
reacted with pleasure when artfully stroked by an adult, the first time
I was made conscious of the alert response the nerve endings there
were capable of. It was 20 years after I was sexually misused
before I understood what my molester had actually done to me:
he had permanently associated my first experience of sexual pleasure
with my having no say in the matter. That, I believe, is the true meaning
of rape."*

Rafael Yglesias [16]

1. What Am I Doing Here?

"Some 100,000 children were required to attend residential schools over the past century in an attempt to rid them of their cultures and languages. The legacy of sexual abuse and isolation among these children has long been cited by Indian leaders as the root cause of epidemic rates of alcoholism, drug addiction and suicide on Canadian reserves."[17]

"Such early abuses lead to a serious distortion in the victim's mind
about what constitutes affection, love, protection and trust.
Often times, the victim will try to repeat
the experience in later life, inviting repetition."
                    (Neil Goldschmidt "explaining" Elizabeth Dunham's brutal rape
                              in Seattle years later.)[18]

"Ye have heard that it hath been said,
thou shalt love thy neighbor, and hate thine enemy.
But I say onto you: Love your enemies, bless them
that curse you, do good
to them that hate you, and pray
for them which despitefully use you and
persecute you."   (Jesus, Sermon on the Mount. Mathew 5:43-44)

I sit here
inside your clanging steel gates
amidst armed guards on this sacred site, Two Rivers
where the Snake enters the Columbia[19]
unsure which of the four doors you'll come through
unsure I'll recognize you

But it is you
for all you've been through
beautiful man of the Niatallchkwa
fullblood of this land

Our brief embrace, ten seconds the instructions scream
from ceiling and walls. The guards watch us.
We sit four feet apart
facing each other

I talk and you talk
my foot keeps touching yours
but it is our eyes that are free.
There is most of all
in the Two Rivers Correctional Institution Visiting Room

looking. Everyone taking in through the eyes
all that's possible, the only thing
that can be taken from here

I would have recognized you anywhere
though now crippled
from the suicide attempt after the verdict

"Easier," you sigh, "than Kamloops
Indian Residential School."

I am here, for you, simple as that, your
sister. Not a serious distortion in my mind, Governor,
          (is this not blaming the victim again?)
but yes, something of repetition.
I am here for us, despite all who won't understand,
who triumph I'm sick, a deer attracted to the headlights.
Inexplicable, how I, raped, violated
by my father, could be supportive of you.
How is it that I still love my father?

The Stockholm Syndrome, they diagnose
though not the Jesus Syndrome.
The battered mate syndrome
though not the Forever vow of marriage
not the for-better-or-worse syndrome, not
Forgiveness

Not the Michael Dorris Syndrome

          the successful Native American (Modoc) writer
          who founded and worked untiringly for children's organizations
          and Indian causes, funded and acclaimed all over the world
          for his heroic campaign
          to inform us of Foetal Alcohol Syndrome

                    *In 1971 Michael Dorris was the first unmarried man in the US
                    allowed to adopt a child. At the end of a long
                    homosexual relationship, he adopted three Sioux infants.
                    Homosexuals are no more likely to abuse their children than heterosexuals.
                    This is simply testimony of Dorris' legal prowess.*

In 1972 Dorris founded Dartmouth College's Native American
Studies Department
one of the first in academia.
Ten years later he married his Chippewa-Turtle Mountain/German
student,
Louise Erdrich. Together
they published, became wealthy, famous, and revered.
She wrote a memoir, the exquisite The Blue Jay's Dance: A
Memoir of Early Motherhood[20]
of birthing one of their three daughters
I used as a guide in my own writing
of the birth of my son[21]

But something was wrong with his adopted Sioux children:
No doubt, their natal mothers
drank.

Dorris won international acclaim for the TV Special
about these children, about Native Americans, their abuse of alcohol.
The Broken Cord *won the 1989 National Book Critics Circle Award*
for General Nonfiction. Erdrich and Dorris both advocated
imprisoning pregnant Indian women who drank.

Like you, Neil Goldschmidt who established the Oregon
Children's Foundation
after announcing to the shock of all Oregon
you would not run for your second term, afraid
the fact of Elizabeth was coming out
Michael Dorris founded Save The Children Foundation
and other such programs

in the name of children, in the name of Indians
in the name of grants, publications, acclaim
"manifest manners" a scholar names it[22]
to hide the fact
to hide his guilt, to appease his shame, to blind himself

that all the while he was sexually molesting his children.
At least this will be the accusation of four of his six
                    children, including one of his
Modoc-Chippewa daughters

maybe even the one whose pregnancy and birth
is so beautifully told in *The Blue Jay's Dance.*

    Remember, poet, a man is innocent until proven guilty

Now I'm forced to consider
The Blue Jay memoir
as fiction, as
lies

to hide the truth
to veil their "house of hell."

As with members of my family
Michael Dorris went to extraordinary lengths
to successfully deceive us. He posed

as a leader on behalf of kids
                    (against their mothers, against their people
Such lengths to which the guilty will go
to hide their crimes
such avenues of exit we allow them
to pull the wool over our eyes
to pull the wool over their own eyes

Like Elizabeth Dunham, Abel Dorris,
Michael's oldest Sioux son
went crazy. The emotional insanity when blackmailed
when the truth is not believed
when no escape to the truth is possible
when shattered parts of the lie
keep multiplying around you

When full memory is not allowed. When full memory
is labeled retardation
as in so many medically profitable diagnoses

Michael Dorris legally declared Abel mildly retarded
from his prenatal exposure to alcohol, not

from the boy's exposure to him

    At the age of 24 Abel
    awaiting the trial he brought
    to testify about the house of hell
    was hit by a car, outside the New Hampshire *Blue Jay* home.
    Some said he was murdered, but the Court ruled
    hit and run

Then Dorris and Erdrich pursued a court case
against their other adopted Sioux son

Jeffrey Sava
who accused them both of child abuse. Jeffrey Sava
testified too
the home he grew up in
was a house of hell

    I hear my uncle
    my father's older brother say of their childhood home
        in Tennessee
    "The terrible things that went on in that house."[23]
    Forbidden words in my house.
    I hear Sava's lawyer say
    "I detest Michael Dorris, he's completely
    evil," and his Sioux daughter, Madeline, testify
    "he raped me repeatedly in childhood."

Jeffrey Sava was their first legal failure
    their first nonsuccess
    but the same year as the successful *Blue Jay*

    sickening the politics behind some successful publishing

I see the literary superstar Michael Dorris again and again
sitting under the flagpole at Seattle's Bumbershoot[24]

apart from us, the poets on the patio
his posture, his aura, my intuition, something
beneath his dark charisma exclaiming shame
though I have heard nothing but acclaim

Am I guilty of projection?
Innocent until proven guilty?
The many mistaken distrusts and accusations
of me
wash over me again

and I see again and again Keintpoos, the Modoc
                    Captain Jack,
Michael Dorris' tribal ancestor
being hung

myself driving around Dorris, California
in search of Keintpoos, in search of the truth

in search of the curse
in search of the land
                    I didn't want to live
                    when they hanged him

Cornered, subpoenaed, about to be exposed
Michael Dorris checked into a motel in New Hampshire
swallowed a bottle of opiates
a bottle of vodka
tied a plastic bag over his head

a shock to the world
        (though this was his second attempt that spring)
which regarded him a hero
like the shock to Oregon of their governor

        Imagine the self hatred
        that enabled him
        to succeed at such self violence

or was it
self love? Self preservation?

Remember he maintained his innocence to the end

Was he too a victim? Modoc,
French, Irish, was he too molested by priests in childhood?

Dear Kha-che-chee I'm here in protest of your being here.
No one should be here.
This is not to say the guilty should not be looked at, held accountable.

In amnesty may we begin to see
in full memory our way out

our child to be hanged

I'm here for myself,
for the little girl I was
for the little boy you were.
I'm here for my father.
I'm here for my son
and for my daughter.
I'm here for all children
now and then

I'm here, o Love
for the sorrow
*

Keintpoos

I wanted to live in Keintpoos' cave of wives.
To lie down with him in his bed. I wanted
to lie down and die

Above me against the sky you called me back.
I didn't want to live when they hanged him.

We wandered east along the border of our two states.
Looking for the Falls of the Klamath, drove through
The Labyrinth of Lava. Hiked down the River of Rocks
to their stronghold, the last stand of the Modoc.

A child stared out from the cave.
Damp, pitch black. It was then
I would have traded all my woman rights, everything
to live those four and a half months
in there with him.

A woman sat on the open ledge when you pointed
west to the Ridge where the Army
gathered and camped. Mt. Shasta
went behind the sky. Further inside
three more. Then suddenly
the cave filled with them. I knew
envy.

The Klamath flows from where the Falls
were dynamited, the land reclaimed.
Where DDT drains the Tule, where salmon.
Where herons, pelicans, grebes, gulls. Where deer. Where Spring
is silent. Where you won't know why
this Hell, where you say you can't.
It's too much pain, too daunting
but dare to ponder why Captain Jack did it. Still see
all sides and claim you love me.

Where can we go now Love but into the collapsed tubes
into the confluence of poisons? Into this ancient eruption.
Into his cave further back where his sons wait.
I study the photo the day before he is hanged. Yes.
I'm in love with him. The day
they are shipped to Oklahoma. I keep
making love with you to make his babies. I'd give my life
for you to know how bad. This man hanging
from the cave opening over us. This child
hanging. Our child to be hanged.[25]

2. Toward Full Memory   Forbidden

When the pioneers arrived
to this last place, the mid-Oregon coast
unsettled for the mile of skeletons
laid out to sand, sea, wind and sun
they settled
by stripping the corpses of their garments
exchanging with traders, the new museums and colleges
for their first American money, throwing the bones
into the Alsea and the sea.

Occasionally, even now a skeleton
in full regalia is found in the dunes.[26]

a.

We met on the dance floor at the Bay Haven. I was taken
by your Indian beauty   (forbidden)   as perhaps you were taken
by my blond. Forbidden.
You told of your two tribes, your mother and father, separate
tribes opposite banks of the Niatallchkwa
the Shuswap, the Lillooet. You were born
a twin. As we danced I felt the umbilical cord wrap us together
brother and sister, two tribes from conception

your long black hair. Your grace and sweetness   your
beauty   our bodies in sync
together from the beginning   (forbidden

      our bodies of violations   (forbidden
      our bodies of desire beyond violations   (forbidden
      our souls to survive   (forbidden

before we could talk, our language of the thousand different tongues
I understood
more than my only tongue, English, my
      broken cord

That night I slept in Psyche, my van
in the harbor parking lot   (forbidden

The next morning, Waldport
only eighteen miles south, but Waldport, a world apart,
astonishingly, you were at my mother's front door

hired the week before to help her with the insulation
of her house just sold

      Beyond you
      standing in her door, north in the dunes
      that place on the beach I've found in my sunset walks, a creek
      that comes down through the big conifers
      from Hidden Lake. Wading it

      to a cutbank five feet high

      of evenly stacked layers, each about two inches thick, seven
                    feet long
      red, gold, blue, purple, black and white layers oozing
      glistening oil
      a little slice of earth, wave-carved, but untouched by us.
      Not bulldozed, developed,
      hacked or hoed, not redone, rearranged, reused, converted for
                    our money plans.
      Only sand and wind and sun and creek water. Only the ocean

      But how can that be? A slice of earth   (forbidden!
      beyond you in my mother's door
      untouched. Mineral, sand
      crystal, bone, shell, what geological process
      created those oil-oozing colored layers?

which will always show in my full memory of you
at her door

      and down in her basement
      my just finished bookpoem
      The Husband Arcane.   *The Arcane of O*
      which ends
      "I ovulate against us."   Forbidden

My mother believes OJ is innocent.
"Those two are murdered, Mama, that's a fact.
Someone, most likely some woman's son
cut the throats of those two."

My mother will sigh of you at her door
we were bound to meet

b.

We have lunch at the Adobe
south in Yachats, my father's favorite place, the last place
he ate out. "He got so sick," she will always tell.

As we eat I see them   (forbidden)   starving
scrambling for fish on the long rockslabs beneath the exploding waves
west and below us in the window
tribes from all over Southern Oregon
herded here last century after the Rogue River Wars.
As we eat I see them drowning.
My eyes can't look at you enough.

You say the Seventh Element and draw the rivers
around Kamloops, British Columbia
the Thompson and the North Thompson.[27]
You say the Native name
Niatallchkwa
the sound of ripples over stone.
You say your name is the sound of water over stone
in the Niatallchkwa   the Shuswap and the Lillooet as one[28]

I draw the Linga Sharira, my Seventh Element
on the white paper tablecloth.
I ask you your birthdate.
"March 25 and my sister's"

the date I dreamed Crazy Horse fifteen years ago
that became my epic poem

"I dream he is my lover.
We lie on the hard ground, beneath a single robe, the marriage blanket….
He takes me all the way into the male world….
He is the one I have waited for, my strange
familiar Oglala….

The danger is great
only if we fail each other"[29]

I don't see that you're involved
with another woman
and her daughter   (forbidden

        I don't examine the glistening colored layers,
        the wave-cut little bluff of the Waldport sand dunes.
        But I look for it every time
        walking by. To believe my eyes. To get beyond the forbidden

the dead laid out, flesh and bones
in full regalia, beads, shells, feathers, animal fur
decomposing human bodies
to the sand and wind and sun and creek   to the ocean
those dazzling colors, bejeweled vestments
lasting longer that human flesh
those 12000 years here
eons before that

c. Looking For You Last Night

"This Indian came who believes in the spirit. He gave an eagle feather to someone. It's an
honor to receive an eagle feather. It's really an honor for a person to give it to you. It's
respected. But that person refused it. That person is a Christian. That wasn't their way."
                                                  Priscilla Hunter[30]

Saturday Sunset, Dec 2, 1995, Bayshore, Waldport, Oregon
my last letter from here, tomorrow we move
from this sand spit of the Alsea souls
laid out in their burial clothes
to the four directions, plus
above and below, laid out
to the wind the water the sand the sun.
This ancient land of the dead

where I have experienced what we talked of, what it is to be
the Seventh Element. How many days, mostly nights
I've walked this beach, usually south to the river
and east up it, sometimes up to the bridge and across it
through the rain and wind, stars and dark night
to Yaquina John Point, the southwest end of the bridge
where Chief Yaquina John relocated to watch over his son
laid here in the dunes across the Alsea. Where they lie
in their death garments to all the universe, now the quicksand
of local lore

Dear Incredibly Beautiful Man of Newport,
as long as I live I will not overcome the pain in your face
early this morning
when I didn't accept your eagle feather

"An Indian ought to have an eagle feather"
you said offering it to me
when I told you of my Cherokee, my Lumbee, my Seminole
when I told you of Ramona and my first love, Ramon

> *mi Kumeyaah*
> *mi Ipai, my Soboba, mi San Pasqual, mi Mesa Grande, mi*
> *Diegueño, mi Mission Indian, all names now for one boy*
> *Ramon, mi first story*

a pain so deep and yet so open, so given, like the eagle feathers
arrayed on the wall over your couch.
Like the wave-cut colored sand layers of the dead.

I trust you understand
what happened to me in that moment.
I would finally be a poet if I could write a poem
of your face in that moment. Face
that believes in spirit.

I was being respectful, principled, spiritual
the opposite of what is regularly
projected about me

as they will accuse (perhaps even you)
the white woman ripping you off

> *I was fearful that in the awe of our new love, you had fallen*
> *beyond wisdom*

> *I am not that woman*
> *but now I feel sick*

> *that I failed you*
> *that sacred (forbidden) moment*

You told of declining
the sacred honor of your people in Canada
to be their chief, to succeed your brother to your hereditary place.
"I'm not ready yet!" you gasped when you told me.
Such irony, maybe self-hatred
in your voice

> *"I'm not ready yet either" I gasped.*
> *My failure of our spiritual meeting   (forbidden*

Now it is 9:45 pm and my mother has gone to bed.
And now I too must. I'm exhausted. Tomorrow we move
back to Ashland. Goodnight
beautiful new friend.

> *P.S.*
> *"I do not know what I may appear to the world*
> *But to myself I seem to have been*
> *Only like a boy playing on the seashore,*
> *And diverting myself now and then*
> *In finding a smoother pebble or a prettier shell than ordinary,*
> *Whilest the great ocean of truth*
> *Lay all undiscovered before me."*

Sir Isaac Newton[31]

d. Six Weeks Later, February 14, 1996, The Paris Theater Portland Oregon *"Sharon Doubiago Takes On OJ Simpson"*[32]

I read from my new book
costumed in a black shiny mini skirt
and back-strapped high heels
my pompadour combed like
Nicole Brown Simpson.

You stand behind me in the blue cotton prayer shirt you made
beads and feathers hanging off.
You blow the beaded bamboo flute

two polarities of America
one behind the other
our incongruity
                 our tragedy
aligned

       How did this performance come about?
       My ongoing Native American theme, yes,
       but it has nothing to do with my bookpoem
       about OJ and Nicole

             though there is the issue of race
             and, as if prescient, the issue of us, of this poem
             the issue of gender
             the issue of abuse
             the issue of innocence and guilt
             the issue of sadomasochism
             the issue of sex
             the issue of love

I won't know for years
that your love, Teanne, is in the audience
having raced up from the coast
       I didn't know you had a lover

             Is she checking on you
             the mother whose daughter has told?

Is she trying to know who to believe, her lover
or her daughter?

A daughter herself, she knows
the man's sexuality. But she wants to believe
her daughter makes things up. Fibs. Lies.
Not you. To whom she gives herself
onto the possibility of a new child.
She can dismiss her daughter's fantasies, just a child.

I, a child, told my mother
and that was our end.
My mother fought for her man, for her marriage, over me,
                    the girl.
I forbade myself knowing this
I didn't know my own story
though that's why all those years later
I was living with her in Waldport.
My soul-longing for her. My being the love
that would not betray her

my being witness
to my father's betrayal of my mother,
made her betrayer
by his betrayal of me.
I knew the depth of horror
but couldn't say it, my Philomela tongue cut out[33]
so as not to know the even greater unbearable, my mother's
                    betrayal
of me

Mute, I would not betray my mother,
make her an orphan again.
But I would never be my mother
who fights for her man
over her daughter. Never
the woman who fights
the other woman, any woman,
for her man.

I love only if love wants me

though never if he is with another
                    if I know, if I am not betrayed

never if he is like my father, never if he wants me
as my father wanted me.

My publishers drove up from Mendocino to bring the just published book.
We didn't rehearse, but your flute seemed perfect
if unrelated to the theme.
What did Teanne see?

There was only one room available that night at the Mallory.
One room with one bed.
I slapped down our draw from the door. This will be okay.
I wasn't looking for sex with you. Not yet anyway.
Never incidental, casual or causal sex for me.
Sharing a bed with you was soul friendship, not lust or desire.

You didn't sleep. You were like a blue volcano
on your back, a frozen mountain in that one bed
a man terrified.
I huddled the wall, my back to you, worried that once again
I've freaked a man. And how weird our performance, my OJ poem,
how weird it must have seemed to the audience, an Indian accompanying
                Nicole.
And for you, how weird my radical friends, my publishers, my new book,
its controversial subject. I didn't dream
you were freaked about your lover

        I didn't know you had a lover

Teanne
and her daughter, Beth

The next morning we had breakfast with my publishers.
She carried on at her most radical, about Judi Bari
and Earth First, the FBI's bombing of them.
I felt you growing tighter. My great friends
frightened you.

We drove south out of Portland, I behind you to the Corvallis exit.
You took off on the ramp, west, not a nod back to me
like all the disappearing men of my life.

Days later you called, "this cannot work." Right then
the Ashland sun pierced my eyes through the window and I wrote
even before we hung up some of the lines in the "Alima" prayer poems
of my next book

> *"if in the roots I get lost*
> *in the clouds, if my trunk, my tusk, my hair, my vulva, my Zebra*
> *tailbone, testicle, protozoa, forgive me Love, I*
> *forgive you Moon your white*
> *disappearing night beneath me …*
>
> *if on me the sun, coming back, your whole self*
> *if the sun goes back…*
> *…*
> *I put on…*
>
> *the Niatallchkwa*
> *song of the ripples over rocks in the creek to the Lillooet*
> *and the Shuswap your mother and father where uncle*
> *betrayed the Okanagan Salish   our eggs*
> *the Chilcotin and the Yalakom plus others on the Gun*
>
> *the sound of waters the ones beneath and never birthed"*

I thought it was my publishers, their radicalness.
My education, publication, success,
the controversial subject of OJ and Nicole. His guilt or innocence.
She, mother of black children, believed the jury's verdict was the correct
             verdict.
I feared the poem itself frightened you, my voice as Nicole, my voice as
             OJ too.
I feared again you felt ripped off and used, an Indian.
I, the poet you thought was a sweet innocent romantic Hallmark versifier
             and rhymer
frightened you. But now I see

Teanne in the audience. You are in bed with me
seeing her, where
o where is she? Now I ponder
you were messing with her little girl,
were cast in deep alarm, both in the prospects of being found out
and in losing access to them. This
cannot work. You had to stay with Teanne
to combat the truth coming out.
You had to prove your love to Teanne, not
commit another infidelity.
You had to stay. Sell your business, everything. Go with her.
If gone, the girl would tell.
Teanne would believe
her child

       as my father knew I would tell my lovers
       the main reason
       even more than their possession of his property
       he hated them

From prison you say of this night
I was honorable, right?
From this night you know, poet
I am an honorable man.

I thought it was just our politics
that freaked you at breakfast.

e. Nine Years Later

My mother dead like my father
and Ramon
I'm in Sea Ranch
on the Northern California Coast
writing at long last the forbidden,
my father's sexual molestation of me as a girl
and my family's complicity

when you are arrested.
Lynn sends me Newport's front page news.
"I'm sorry to tell you this, Sharon"

Man Arrested on Multiple Counts of Sex Abuse

A former Newport resident was arrested this week on an outstanding warrant involving multiple charges of sex abuse.

Jack Retasket, 54, who currently lists his address as Cache Creek, British Columbia, Canada, was arrested in Lincoln County on April 6.

A warrant for Retasket's arrest had originally been issued in January 2003, but when that warrant still had not been served as of February of this year, it was recalled, amended, and reissued by the judge.

Retasket was then arrested and lodged in the Lincoln County Jail. He faces five counts of Sexual Abuse 1 and one count of Sexual Penetration with a Foreign Object. The sexual abuse is alleged to have occurred on a number of occasions between January 1995 and December 1996, all involving the same victim, who was a female under the age of 12.

Retasket remains in custody at the jail, with bail set at $250,000. His next scheduled court appearance is a pre-trial hearing on April 26.

I write to you, care of Lincoln County Jail
or was it to your lawyer, Jeff Ouderkirk?
Your phone calls and letters start coming.

        You will tell of looking
        those years for my van
        parked outside the Sylvia Beech Hotel
        where sometimes I slept

        The Sylvia Beech with its rooms
        decorated in the themes of writers.
        I named my Psyche parked there
        The Sharon Doubiago Room   (forbidden

your grace and sweetness   your mystical
humor   your beauty   intelligence   our bodies dancing in sync
from the beginning

the Cord not broken
when you drew the rivers (o, river of my mouth

when we talked the thousand different lost tongues
(o, river of the stars
when I drew the Linga Sharira
when we danced beyond the law
when we talked of what it is to be the Seventh Element
when you explain again

> *"The Seventh Element is*
> *the center of the circle*
> *from all directions.*
> *Everything*
> *is connected to the center,*
> *we see from there,*
> *we are balanced there,*
> *and should always know to return to that sacred spot.*
> *If not we're lost. Sadly, most never are aware of this.*
>
> *The East is yellow,*
> *the place of sunrise,*
> *all birth begins there,*
> *a place of beauty*
> *and curiosity*
> *where we unfold and begin to grow,*
> *are well-protected,*
> *innocent.*
> *One of the first understandings*
> *is the love we are given.*
> *It is good there.*
>
> *The South is red, warm, and quick,*
> *the time of youth,*
> *where we're reaching out*
> *expanding our conscientious-learning to care for*
> *the younger and respecting the older.*
>
> *The West is black, night—adulthood, guiding the adolescent.*
> *A busy time preparing for winter. Protecting the young and old.*
>
> *The North is white, the peaceful time,*
> *story telling time, time to enjoy the works we've done."*[34]

f. **The Seventh Element But Hate Still in Waldport**

"The only good Indian is a dead Indian," General Philip Sheridan

"I hate Indians!" His hatred
still comes, high
tide. Ripped water back. Bizarre
this last decade of the 20th Century
though a tidal wave from Alaska
destroyed this waterfront town
not long ago

I want to kneel into his curse at the end of the bar
in prayer, plead why? The dead beneath the lodge
turn over, cry
if they could, the bones on which my country
are propped, this great grandson
of the killers, the whites, this property owner, is why, how
it comes down. Ownership. Prejudice

> *when they arrived*
> *this last place, not settled*
> *for the mile of skeletons*
> *laid out to sand, sea, wind and sun*

But I have to walk the long night beach back.
Like the wives of genociders
on orders of the California governor
the three designated dates
I know better than to confront him.
I can only hide you
to secure my passage north through the dunes
the sand of flesh, the wild waves of souls
to my mother

*

Mass Execution of Aboriginal Children of the Mohawk Residential School, Brantford, Ontario, 1943

when you were five
> *when you were kidnapped from your family and imprisoned in*
> *Kamloops*
when I was two
> *when the Nazis*
when Babi Yar
> *when I was five months*

when the infamous Mush Hole mass execution of children
of Brantford Mohawk Indian Residential School
run by the Church and Crown of England

when they lined up the children next to a big ditch
and shot them
so they fell into the ditch

when some of the kids were still alive
when they shoveled the dirt on top of them. Buried them alive
on land occupied by the Canadian Army
at its Basic Training Camp Number 20

when on this earth   when in time
we are breathing
the same air they are breathing, the killers
when their victims
when Time

as me, you
as them, inside us
we breathe

all things
connected   as above
so below

when we were children, prisoners
of the Church's concentration camp

inspired by the Nazis
who were inspired by the American Holocaust
when the 19 million Indigenous Americans disappeared
when Hitler found his model
in Andrew Jackson
who sent the Cherokee on the Trail of Tears
against Congress's vote
when Hitler wrote
"I model my Solution
on the American Solution
of its Natives"

    "How native American
    the line
    to the shower, now
    there's an archetypical image…"[35]

when the wives
hid you in their pantries, under their beds
when their husbands on orders of California's governor
were hunting you down to kill

    when your parents, kidnapped, impoverished prisoners in Kamloops
    surviving on mush
    when they heard[36]

    when "infamous,"
    when they stood us

    Jews and Indians, Africans, Muslims, Chinese, when et al
    this archetypical image
    when I was a white girl
    burned at the stake

       when my father

       when the spirit breaks
       when the tar of despair

the quicksand of the buried bodies
the sorrow
the soul
denied

when all you have is your secret sex
when finally alone
the only sacred place
all that you have, your self

when the self triumphs

and this is God

3. Kamloops Indian Residential School

Five, hand in hand, on each side of your mother
you and your twin sister, Wendy, Sweet
Medicine Woman, arrived
at the five-story, stone monster
erected on the shrub plain of British Columbia
both of you sobbing, no, no, don't leave us here!
But your mother and father, Shuswap and Lillooet
opposite sides of the Niatallchkwa

> which begat Restasket
> which becomes Fraser, where the Yalakom
> enters from the center of earth
> thousands and thousands of years
> before the British, before Columbus

were brought to this monster also at five.
Given to the black robed monsters too.
Against the law
not to put your children in Catholic Indian Residential School.
Against the law
for Native American children to attend public school.

Weaved together as you came into being from them, wrapped together
with the cord, inseparable in the small non-insulated Reservation house
—in winter each's fire, in summer each's mirror—
you lose her too
on entering Kamloops Indian Reservation School

ordered first thing to put out your tongue
for lashing with a razor strap[37] embedded with steel strips
and again every time you spoke your language
"and the strap used to whip us for other wrongs, beat our bottom bare.
On our hands palm up, and our wrists."

"We weren't allowed to dress as Indians
but every Christmas we were dressed as Santa Clauses
and paraded down the main street of Kamloops."

"The few times I saw Wendy in chow line
she was so small and afraid, too alone.
She stood at the center of a blurred vacuum.
She always tried to smile but it was too difficult.
I was so happy to see her, once or twice
we couldn't hold it and we cried.
There she was, six or eight feet away, my blood, my
twin and we couldn't touch."[38]

When your twin is hit on the head by a nun
she's sent home to die.
But, heartbroken, hearing gone in one ear, she revives.
Your parents flee with her and your four younger siblings
across the border to Oroville Washington
making the apple harvest
putting her in public school
but leaving you behind

*

4. The Rape

9:54 pm, April 15, 2006, Two Rivers Correctional Institution, Umatilla, Oregon

It is spring, warm. I live on the fifth story of the school, really the attic, so most of the light comes in through a dozen or so dormers. My bed is in the light and the bathrooms are inside of the right angle. I loved to look out the dormers. I could see town across the river, four train tracks and two-lane roads. I saw my good friend Douglass from Chase trying to get to a soccer game. I miss him. One winter he just stepped in front of the train in Chase. Sometimes it is hard to imagine what people thought, them zipping around the metropolis in those fancy cars and a city full of light....

The dorm holds nearly one hundred and seventy five of us. The building is shaped like the letter L, but with both sides equal, the girls on the other side. There are two ways out, the fire escape and the stairwell.... Our dorm is shared with first to fourth grades called the juniors. The next level was the intermediators, 5th to 8th. And seniors below that....

The people who are not ordained were teachers, disciplinarians, or workers. They are in the mission field from Europe and Ireland as well as Britain, training us to assimilate into society. Some have boys, maybe girls that attend our school, and are living in nice homes on school property. The two families I need to speak of are the Openhiemers and Palzois from Germany.

The abuse came about in steps. When you walk down, the levels have hallways both directions, with a disciplinarian on each level. On the third floor is where Brother Shirley lives in a medium-sized room adjacent the stair well.

There are two Openhiemers boys and one Palzoi.[39] Demanding, obnoxious and overpowering, they are allowed on each level to do whatever, mostly harassing us juniors and smaller intermediators. They are nasty and gang-up to harass. They are mean.

One day I was coming downstairs and they were on the third floor and wouldn't let me pass, they pushed me around into the void beneath the stairs, started to hold me down and tickle me. Pretty quick I'm on my knees and two took turns to pretend they are fucking me. In about five minutes Brother Shirley catches them. He scolds them and slaps me, it feels like it's my fault. He wore black robes unless he went to town. Earlier he'd pat my head or mess up my hair, everyone tried to avoid him. Within a few days he would pull me against him, I knew he didn't wear pants, because he'd moved me around in front of him and I could feel him hard. It feels like he is seeking me out. I felt dirty. Everyone called him Hawkeye. He was everywhere and missed nothing. I hated him, he's probably about forty, bald on top. The hair on the sides was shiny from the stuff he put on it and slicked back. Pock marks, bushy eye brows, evil-looking squinted eyes behind glass. It is difficult to tell where he is looking. I wasn't the only one he harassed. But it feels like it's my fault. When he started I thought he was playing around, I felt less scared. The first time I hate that he rubs himself. I could feel him about the middle of my back. He'd stop when he heard people, he'd push me away and tell me to get up or downstairs, this was in the hallway....

When he caught those boys I think twice, he asked what they were doing and if I liked it. I'm just scared.

Brother Murphy has a small room with windows to see the dorm. He is from Scotland. He would read us a chapter of different tales standing on a chair under the light. I liked his accent. Our beds touch from head to toe, bunched tight, where he could walk through and wake us up two at a time, because we'd wet the bed. Brother McAllister who'd be there in the morning would make us wrap our wet sheets around our head with nothing else on and make us stand in front of everyone. He'd ridicule us. I hated it because I wet the bed more often than some. They make sure everyone knows if I did wrong, but nobody, what no one, laughed or mocked us, they just felt sorry for us. If you fight you have to wear gloves and box in front of everyone. When we're both exhausted and given up, they'd make us keep punching. That happened in our inside room where we had cubbies to keep coat, boots and stuff. My number was 54 and printed on everything we wear, jeans and a flannel shirt, that were washed Saturdays. I hated that part too because afterwards I began to shit my pants and would take the underwear under the gym through a torn vent. When clothes came back I'd have to make up lies about what happened to them and most of the time I'd just say I didn't know. It was ugly because it was hard sometimes really hard not to do that in my jeans and always feel like I stink.

When it's too hot we could wear shorts and I was running down stairs and got caught. First Brother Shirley bent over and scolded me, he made me go into his room. I thought I'd be spanked by his razor sharpening strap on my hands and arm that hurt, if you try to pull your hands out of the way you got two more, if you swore or spoke in your language the steel cut your tongue, he made me face the wall in front of his big ugly chair that was brown and like crushed velvet only longer. There was a bowl of marbles he took from kids on the shelf on my left. The other was the wall the door was on. He began yelling at me, told me I'm in trouble and would be punished. That room smelt bad. If you move you are going to get it. He always keeps the strap by the door so we see it. Then he took it down and hit me, that's for running when you know not to. This one is for what you did under the stairs. You know what I'm talking about. Why did you do it? Do you like that because it makes you feel good? That's wrong. When he hit me I nearly fell off the chair, then he told me to drop my shorts and get up on the chair. Where's your underwear, you have to wear them all the time. He hit me for that, then he started asking and talking about what happened under the stairs and spanks me hard. It hurt bad because I didn't have my underwear. I started crying hard. He grabbed my ankle, the left one really hard and told me I better shut up, be quiet unless you want more. Then he rubbed my butt where he hit me, almost like he was sorry. Then he talked about the stairs. You want me to do that so you learn a lesson. I was crying hard but quiet as I could, the kind when my body is jerking and can hardly breathe, sounds move like the swells of the ocean and so did my thoughts. Objects seem ten times their size and were right in my face. It was hard to hear what he was saying, my hands slipped off the back of the seat because they were wet, he yelled at me for that, he said get back up be quiet or I give you more. It's hard not to slip when I jerked he grabbed me by my hips and Shut up you like what you did under the stairs. Then he started to rub my hips and butt, his hands were big and hairy, and wet.

He was quiet for a while, when he talked it was like a yelling whisper. I could hear when he hung the strap back up, because there are steel strips in the belt for when you finish sharpening.... He was getting some lotion by his sink. I tried to run for the door and tripped because my pants were around my legs. Now he locked the door. He spit on his hands and rubbed it on the tip, then he poured some yellowish lotion on his hand and began to stroke himself, then he made me do it, it was warm and hard, my hands were shaking and seemed too small to reach around him, he grabbed my hand and squeezed till it hurt, my wrist was in the wrong position, I hurt myself trying to pull away, he wouldn't let me go and just stroked harder and faster. I'm not even eight. I think I was chattering. I told you to obey me why didn't you?.... I'm scared to no end, I can't even cry. You always make God mad, obey us or you'll burn in hell forever. I finally yelled but he just grabbed my mouth shut and said Now you're asking for it he spun me around bent me over the armchair and spit on his hands, he tipped me way forward and spread my cheeks and poured lotion on me and around my bottom then put my knees on the arm rest and bent me over hard, I was scared and could barely hear him, he kept talking about the stairs and started to push against me, at first slow then harder, he was really hard I said I want to go, I won't do.... He made me promise or it will be worse. Be quiet, remember your promise or I'll get your brother. His robe was gone and he leaned on me and moved like he wanted to feel everywhere with his cock. I was freaking by then he was quiet and said be quiet stop breathing like that. I can remember I held my breath hard to be quiet when I put my head down I could see his big white hairy legs. If you tell you'll really get hurt. All this time he's dragging his cock all over my butt and legs. He said you'd better not tell if you know what's good for you.

Then he spread my cheeks past hurt and put his cock in me. I fell over and just tried to get away. He just jerked me back up. He hurt me like an explosion way inside whenever he moved. I couldn't breathe, when I tried to yell he whopped the back of my head really hard. It was really hot I'd spit something on his chair when he rammed me, I was choking on nothing, it looked ugly on the chair I don't know how long he fucked me I could see between my legs and blood was going down. It just hurt so bad and all I could hear was inside my head. I felt ashamed I sweat like crazy, everything hurt everywhere, I just gave up when he finished he pulled out and tried to close me back up by pushing my cheeks together hard. I got bruised. I can't remember feeling anything but I remember it was like I was hearing and thinking of everything at once. When I tried to get away he yanked me back into the chair. I felt delirious all I could hear then was his ugly voice making sure I wouldn't tell. He told me to touch his cock, when I wouldn't he grabbed my hand and wrapped it around him and yelled get myself off of him. It felt really ugly it was ugly and hard and skinny. I put my head down just crying hard but quiet. He grabbed my head and made me look at him, his whole white body looks like he's an ape or something black and hairy. Then he grabbed my hand around him hard his fingers were big, his hands are big he made my fingers stroke him then he pushed me back in the chair and he looked more evil. He said you see what I mean if you tell I'll do it more if you tell. Your brother, both of you will get it only worse. Remember your promise or else. He was cleaning himself off with an ugly towel, then he picked up my shorts to finish and threw them at me. I put them on as fast as I could. I was skinny. Then he yanked me right up to his face and said remember what I told you, he let go and I felt like I had no legs, he put me in the chair, sit still. He put pants and shirt on, glared at me every little while, he washed his hands in his sink and gave me his glass with water. I wanted it but couldn't swallow and it fell out. I hurt so bad everywhere. My butt hurt like screaming, I didn't think I could walk, felt like he was still in me, my stomach hurt, now nothing would come out. I felt like the water inside me was moving too slow. I sweat so bad it was running off my face, my mouth was dry and hurt I could feel my inside like it's torn up, it felt like my eyes couldn't be wet anymore. I felt like a little bug trying to be seen by a giant. Like I was in another world and couldn't get back. Like it happened a minute ago. I feel strange right now. I'm crying and feel like I'm a little shiny black bug with a weird mouth and tentacles. You can hardly see. Opaque. When it was over I tried hard to think why he did that and the Openhiemers. I had a nail in my cubby and stuck it in the broken light switch to die in our big bath room down stairs. Later I cut my hair weird and scratch my face to look different, when my brother saw me all I could do was lie, fast. Maybe I looked like a girl or maybe I'm different and maybe been born with confused genes, maybe my twin is messed up too. Maybe I was too feminine and they see that even that young. I bleed for awhile and am tender and burning. So am guilty for that, at times I'd be terrified. I'm not even eight.... He tore up my insides, for a while I gave my food away, I couldn't and didn't want to shit,... it hurt too bad to wipe myself. I was afraid I walked so weird, that my brother could tell what happened. I stopped bleeding in about four or five days. I threw my underwear under the gym during that time, I've had nightmares about that one torn vent, that I would have to crawl and retrieve them, or they would know they were mine when they'd find them, because my number 54 was on them. I almost immediately began to wet my bed. When I messed my pants I still hid them there...

Garry, my older brother told me if anyone does wrong to me he'd kill them. And the fucker threatened Garry. I have lied to Garry about this for so long, Sharon, I love both of you deeply, maybe he led me to you, to have someone to trust. The lie of a little brother was still the right thing, the option would have been worse, to me.

Weekly, on Saturday, we had to go to confession, I never told the truth, as a matter of fact, I'd lie to get out of there. When I look back, I see this lonely scared skinny kid, that had no place to go if I ran, my parents were stateside, they were to blame, they took my sis and left me to this. Everything I did was revolved around this, like the center of my fucking life. All the while the nuns and priests saw me as altar boy material, that can't refuse them, so they taught me the rituals, told me it is sacred, I learned the Latin of the Masses, high and low. This numb guilty Catholic boy in these starched angelic lace pullover absolute white shirts worn over a black robe, each time I did it I was to go deeper into hell. I knew that, and could feel him watching me, even though I never looked. What did he think when he saw me, I know, this timid never tell good boy that he had rammed my sin up my ass without any guilt or remorse.

My handwriting here is atrocious, I don't want to correct, much less to reread this and want to seal it before I do, I know I will have many after thoughts. I'll write them down. Before I want to say this. I know I've used that about the femininity side, as an excuse, I've used as an excuse to not feel guilty about my fascination of lingerie, most of all panties, the excuse allowed me to buy panties and use them to masturbate, enjoy and relax. I've been alone so much of my life. I love the fantasy, it was a relief but I've always ended up feeling guilty. I could be the oddest person you met. I don't want to scare you away. I'm getting foolish. There is another letter somewhere, this came from your student exercise. Thank you thank you thank you, I can't show my appreciation enough. I love you so so much, Jack

*

5. The United States of America

When I finally got to my family in Oroville
we lived in this house in the apple orchard.
I tried public school, I'd ride the bus
get off and leave, not entering.
I went from being an A student to much less.
The white kids were mean and ugly
I couldn't believe how ugly
from Missouri and Oklahoma
and the other half from Canada.

There was a white girl,
blond, blue-eyed like you, her eyes
were intense. I walked her home from school
carrying her books just like in the movies.
Suddenly her brother-in-law was there, she hid me in the closet.
I heard what he yelled about me.
"He might be the greatest guy in the world
but he is nothing but a god-dammed Indian.
To be seeing him is plain fucking wrong." He
threatened her.

That was the first time I heard that about me
from the others not Catholic, not nuns and priests.

So a job instead of school.
Babysitter. I was thirteen, she was ten.
I felt guilty from the beginning
but couldn't resist the sensation
the delicious secret between us.

Recently I sought her out, apologized.
She's married now to one of my brothers.
She said it was okay. It's what we did. We were kids.
I wasn't hurt. Her eyes are still intense, her name
is your name.

My mother died. Diabetes
killed her. Sometimes I think
apple pesticide.

I was fourteen.
They brought in the medicine woman.
She did things in the bedroom.
My mother was screaming in our language.
She was really sick.
Took her three days.
I thought I was being punished.
I got really scared.
Everything went wrong.
My father fell apart.
I felt like I was getting blamed.
That's when I took off. I knew I would never come back.
I left with everything in a cardboard box.

I lived in apple pickers' cabins for about a year.
Paid by the tree, that's how I survived.
I'd stash my box in different places while looking for work or food.
In our myth the great Chief Sweetwater
was Keeper of the Box.
One day I hid it behind a garage, next to garbage.
When I came back for it the box was gone. Light
was what was in the Box.

I got a job in the warehouse
putting apples in the box to be shipped.
My second year in Wenatchee I took off
with the carnival. I ended up
all over the northwest. All the counties
that touch the Pacific.

Then Garry, my older brother graduated
so I started following him around.
We lived together in pickers' cabins.
Garry took care of me and loved me, my parent
more than anyone, really the only one my whole life.
He's still the most important.

He was drafted for Vietnam. I hitchhiked to Fort Lewis
where he was in training.
I moved to Puyallup to be close, worked in a door factory.

Did odd jobs. Then he was shipped to Camp Pendleton.
He asked me not to follow so I didn't.
When he told me it was time to go to Vietnam things got tough. I knew
he'd be killed. I'd be truly alone. But he returned
got cancer instead, suffered
long slow death from Agent Orange. Garry died
on this morning I write this, February 23, in 1990.

For thirty years I made Newport my home. Ha! I built that town!
I had my blacksmithing business, welding, insulation, metal works.
I coached basketball, I worked for the Reservation. I married Tina
and had two children.

The card you sent of the fishing vessel, I know that boat
and its twin named the Pacific Rim.
The Pacific Rim and the Pacific Hooker were built shortly after I was
                    shrimp fishing.
I installed air intake to their engine rooms, to help them run cooler.
I miss that city always, and think about skippering
someone's two million dollar machine and the risk they took on me, what
an experience, so long ago, but dear to my heart.

I was never in trouble, one DUI in 1974.
Thirty years almost from that day
they arrested me and found that, my "record."
They gave me the same number. All along
I was in their system.

After all those years I'd finally made it home to Canada.
I got home in '02 after spending too much time alone in Newport,
I nearly drank myself to death. No fun at all.
I wanted help. I went to a Native treatment center
in S.E. B.C near Cranbrook. That was 15 months ago, so far
it's working. When I was there I watched a video
on the effects of Residential School and its trauma.
I found out there were centers to deal with that too, so I jumped on it
and ended up a client through two five week programs at Nanaimo out
                    on Vancouver Island.
I only wish this could have happened years ago. I know
I'm a survivor and what happened to me

happened to me. It is not my fault.
The entire year was the best learning/healing year of my life.

I came back from Canada to do the right thing.
You'd have thought
I was a terrorist the way they handled me
at the border.
Six people with guns drawn.

       Your March 25 Crazy Horse, Love Jack
          April 20, 2004, Lincoln County Jail, Newport, Oregon.

                    (from your first letter to me)

         *

6. Awaiting Trial: The Autobiography of the Soul

Tell me, Oh tell me, Soul, of Teanne.
Remind me of my gullibility

Tell me O Soul, who the other woman is
Tell me what gullibility is

When Teanne's job at the casino ended
so did the relationship. You'd sold your business
to accompany her. "Her trap"
you said recently, the only time
I've heard from you that sexist blame, though years now
imprisoned in that violent all-male environment.

"Her trap."
You had to stay with her
to combat the truth coming out?

She was a trap
laid by you?

Am I assuming
you're guilty?

You are innocent
until proven guilty

Teanne and Beth moved to L.A.
In high school, Beth's teacher
assigned Autobiography. Beth wrote "In Oregon
things weren't so good. Something happened in Oregon."
As required by law, the teacher asked her what happened.
Her mother's boyfriend died, that's one thing.
She must have indicated more. Maybe
she was reading The Oregonian about the Governor.
As required by law, the teacher called the police.

When the officer arrived Beth protested
"I made it up, I was writing fiction."

> *I took my father's side*
> *though I hated what he did*
> *and continued to do to me*
> *I protected him*

He drove her home.
She explained to her mother
"I made it up, I was writing fiction."
She will maintain this at the trial
and her mother, Teanne, will testify
"I have nothing bad to say about Jack Retasket."

Poetry is the voice of the soul.
We are prisoners barred from our selves.
We are kept from our true story.
This is soul violation.

A writer must go deeper
into the true story, the taboo stories.
We must find ways to do this

to ward off their rules, their bars, their knives
to cut out our tongues.
How to remember. To not accept
the current scientific (political) decree: our memories
are suspect, fiction.

We must be more afraid of not knowing the self
than knowing the self and sharing.
We own everything that happened to us.
It's our story, it's all we have.[40]

The endless *I* quotes
of the great writers
counter the ego-forbidden clichés
their laws against our self-knowing
that keep us imprisoned, keep us suffering
writer's block

"I went to the woods because I wished to live deliberately,
to front only the essential facts of life, and see
if I could not learn what it had to teach, and not,
when I came to die, discover
that I had not lived."[41]

Now with your arrest I learn in still another way
that to write autobiography, memoir, to open
in therapy, as you did in Canada
could require the police to be called

    Beware, beware
    of telling the truth

        Beware of knowing the truth

      Beware, in America, in therapy, in Creative Writing
      beware in writing your autobiography
      you better write fiction, you better deny, you better
      lie

      and this is why poetry continually evolves
      to the obscure. In academia
      education is paid mainly by parents.
      Their children, your students better not
      write autobiographies. They better not
      tell the truth, better not tell
      what happened. They better not
      remember.

No charges were filed then
but the new law says
even when the accuser reneges
the police are required
to continue pursuit of the accused

        This is not my mother's country, innocent
        until proven guilty, the one she taught this country is founded on
        (her father escaped from jail, on the run, in hiding)
        This is not innocent "beyond a shadow of doubt"

Seven years later, that cop
who came to the L.A. high school and took Beth's statements
vacations on the Oregon coast
and as required by law
takes up again the pursuit of you

Was that "officer" reading Andrew Vachss' popular cop books?
Did they meet in Newport?

*

7. The Trial

"But I'm not guilty," said K. "There's been a mistake. How is it even possible for someone to be guilty? We're all human beings here, one like the other." "That is true," said the priest, "but that is how the guilty speak." Franz Kafka, *The Trial*

"He's not a hit man. But he shares the same religion I do, which is revenge." Andrew Vachss, Horror Online[42]

"The sadist and masochist are one person." Susan Griffin, *Pornography and Silence*

a.

As you go to trial
a Diocese of Oregon
is found guilty of sexual abuse
of its residential school kids
and the Archbishop of Portland files for bankruptcy[43]
for hundreds of previous claims (and hundreds more to be filed as a result),
the first Catholic diocese to file for bankruptcy

> three months after your arrest
> two months after the Governor's confession

Why did this not help you? Why in fact
may have condemned you. Lynn
wrote:

> "Andrew Vachss—it rhymes with tax—and his wife Alice
> actually live in Newport, hang out with Judge Branford, Jack's judge
> whose son he coached, they're
> best friends. The Vachss are writers from New York.
> He writes murder/police detective novels
> based on child abuse.
>
> He wrote Megan's Law! Did you see him on the cover of Parade
> Magazine,
> his lovely eye patch, shaking hands with President Clinton?
> Andrew Vachss is considered the expert on child abusers, flies
> all over giving talks
>
> has no sympathy for abusers whatsoever, believes
> they cannot be rehabilitated, believes
> they should spend the rest of their lives in prison. No
> mercy

Your sympathy for your father
would not go over well with him

though weird his books—simplistic.
Too too—the rightwing fascist approach
put them away and throw away the key.
He ran a prison in New York, he was the warden.
His books, always a convoluted sexual angle. Classic
S&M. He himself describes his fictitious hero
as having a pathological hatred
for those who prey on children.
Never admits
what happened to him in childhood."

b. **Getting Ready To Walk Free**

You believe to the last hour you'll be found innocent. A big issue,
what you're going to wear. Someone ironing your suit.
Your day of liberation after six months. You believe
you are innocent.

> *"Judge Thomas O. Branford, we know each other, I coached his son in basketball!*
> *Jeff Ouderkirk, my lawyer, is considered the best, he's planning to run for Governor."*

"They offer me a deal, for one third of the time
the Diminished Capacity tack
but I won't take a deal. I'm not going to have anything to do
with their allegations against me

because nothing happened.
There was no danger.
I'm going to sit down and write it."

But the two polygraphs
proving your innocence
aren't allowed in court

Your whole case based on being a truthteller
but you admit the small lie
you told Teanne
"I don't want her to think I would harm Beth in anyway."

Your little lie of compassion
proves you are a liar

> Lesson # 1 in Law School
> *when the defendant*
> *bases his case on the Truth,*
> *maintains he's telling all, maintains he's a truthsayer*
> *the classic rebuttal then*
> *is to show the defendant is a liar*

> ### c.

Your trial should have been moved
out of Lincoln County.
You were unable to obtain a fair trial.

Andrew Vachss, *Parade Magazine*'s leading expert
on child abuse, whose religion is revenge,
is a good friend of your judge. This
is a conflict of interest

and Alice Vachss, head—now, then, or both?—
of the major organization
for child abuse in Newport, the whole County

and your ex, Tina, mother of your children,
now head of the Siletz Tribal organization
federally funded for child sexual abuse
now, then, or both?

So many shady connections. Manifest manners.
Smoke and mirrors, this railroading

> I will sit outside Newport's post office, across
> from the four story cement jail and see
> there are no windows
> on the world's most beautiful coast. This
> is inhuman cruelty, a form of torture

*"Many prisoners have attempted to make a small hole to see outside
since the windows of the jail were sandblasted
following community complaints that prisoners had better ocean views
than the town's law-abiding citizens. These go on their records
as escape attempts."*

d. Abolish All Prisons

*"The prison system is evil
but what do we do
       with psychopathic killers
       those who would do violence
          to others?*

*The prison system
made by the S&M of our culture
needs to be changed*

*but still
what do we do
in the meantime
with psychopathic killers?"*

*

When I Forget You Are Innocent, Love

Better that all the guilty go free
than one innocent man is found guilty.
My mother lectures me every afternoon
home from the Fifth and Sixth Grades
healing herself in her bubble bath
her red-pink nipples bobbing in the Tide.
America is founded on this principle.
This is America's greatness.

After a year her escaped father was caught, retried
found innocent by way of self-defense.
Guy Henry Clarke. That redheaded Irish Cherokee
she never labeled our grandfather. He was her
father. This is the greatness
of America

8. Suicide *(L. sui: of oneself)*
"The West is black, night—adulthood…"

This final day, your day of liberation after six months
the day before my son's birthday
you call seven times awaiting the verdict.
And then, "I'll never walk outside again."
I hear heckling behind you

The next day you tell me who you're leaving your things to, your clothes,
your car, your tribal things, your eagle feathers.
I object. You say again "I'll never walk outside again."

"My lawyer, Jeff Ouderkirk—he says he knows you,
you were at his wedding—he promised
to visit me Saturday and Sunday.
I got our major witnesses down here both Saturday and Sunday, but Jeff
                didn't show.
I was told there'd be a pre-sentence investigation.
There is no such pre-sentence investigation, this is Measure 11.
Oregon's the only state in the country with it. Three strikes and you're out? Well,
one strike in Oregon. The court wouldn't allow the two polygraphs I passed!
To think I could have stayed in Canada.

I came back because it was the right thing to do.
I was being honorable.
I believe there's a difference between honesty and being honorable.
Someone who's honest will live within the letter of the law. Someone
who's honorable will live within the spirit. But Jeff let me know

there is no hope. Ever. There is no chance. At a minimum, 200 months, 17 years
if they choose to run the charges concurrently. I'll be 71.
35 years if they run them consecutively. I'll be 89.
To think there are people
who live this way, do this for a living.
I can't believe it, institutionalized at the beginning of my life by one nation
and institutionalized at the end by another. Two nations.

I have no idea where I'm going. Tomorrow afternoon.
Inmates tell me Coffee Creek, wherever that is. Ontario, Pendleton, Salem.

There is something on the ballot now, because taxpayers are realizing the
                burden of Measure 11.
Ha! I've been a taxpayer right here for thirty years.
But there's no hope. I have to accept. This is election year.
They all want to be reelected."

Then you're back again in Kamloops Residential Indian School,
you and your twin sister
being delivered to the big granite building.
You cite again your poem, "Go Home!"

You ask me to write a letter to the paper
to the citizens of Newport,
"please tell them I am the man they thought I was."
I do, though the newspaper does not publish it.
I write the vow for the beginning of *My Father's Love:*
guilty or not, I will spend the rest of my life
fighting this travesty. Imprisonment
is not the path out of this evil.
A mutual friend will say if he had known
he would have tacked my letter and vow
to every telephone pole in town.

The late September sun shines
like the Golden Rule on the Pacific Ocean
this mansion I'm caretaking
to finally write the book on my childhood rape
the ongoing molestations of my father, the emotional blackmails
and complicities of my mother and sister.

"I could have stayed in Canada," you cry again. "I came back
to do the right thing."
The catcalls, the threats grow as you gasp, "I'm frightened
I am so frightened,
and it's going to get worse
when I hang up"

the crime you're found guilty of
the lowest of the low
the jailed with the same hierarchical sadomasochism
as the jailers

My male friends will triumph too
with heckling lust in their voices
how they'd torture to death any and all molesters
and oh, what they'd love to do to my father

your voice dissolving now
in terror and panic inside me
writing my book at last
opening to the light in the box
and there you are, my Brother, my Native, my Soul Mate
Chief Sweetwater
condemned to their box without light

"Even so, there are things
Innocence   Purity   The Truth

Beth and Teanne are innocent

I am innocent. We
are innocent."

Then you are flying again over Waldport, that time
your friend took you up. The beauty of the world.
You are drawing again the confluence of rivers out from Kamloops.
I'm drawing again the Linga Sharira
I promise you I won't cry

but inside tearless emptiness, there is panic
for the panic in your voice, the coma
you don't tell me you'll soon be in

and I open as that day I opened in greatest pain
to birth my son, today's degree of sun
setting on the Pacific horizon
his body-ripping, traumatizing labor

opening me to the question of God, the question
of my girlhood faith in Jesus and who
the human is, my body's contractions

opening to Christianity's psychic and legal blackmail
identical to what I was subjected to
by my father and family

> *Imagine my son*
> *reading about his beloved grandfather.*
> *Writing my truth*
> *will take from him*
> *the single reliable male in his life*

All week before I learn
I feel you shattering
in your cell, sobbing
as you did in Fifth Grade
caught in a lie, their
blackmail, impossible
not to lie

> *Nothing but a goddamn Indian, you were taught*
> *to lie and deceive, the only survival*
> *for the soul*

I fall again and again off the ocean's black horizon.
Your face comes up on the line, your lips
murmuring to me through sore and pulsating night, your flaming mouths
against my dark skin. I wake
crying

Then fall again off the blackest edge
my face of tears
you must not see

> *"So right after we spoke that day I followed through*
> *with a plan I had*
> *should things turn sour. I got to the second tier*
> *in our pod. I thought of him*
> *getting up on the rail. I reached as far as I could to the lower rail*
> *"This is for you mother fucker!"*
> *and dove head first*
> *pulling myself downward as hard as I could*
> *to increase the impact. And I saw his face, I saw him*

in the bottom rung of hell
which put me here, I saw him, his whole being
as I propelled myself, head first
down the passage

I expected my neck to snap and I'd be gone.
Five days later I woke up
in Oregon State Prison hospital in Salem.
A lot had changed. I looked eighty."

*

9. The Last Time I Saw You

"Remembering is the release of deferred feeling, blocked receptions of crucial experiences that were paralyzed from consciousness in order to survive, but that still reside in the psyche to be either raised by courage or left as poison in the soul. If there [is] a savior… Memory across the gulf of forgetting is that savior, not in the bonds of form that become fascism, the Law."
William Ray[44]

"Somebody killed those two, Mama, that's a fact. Most likely, some mother's son."

You knock on Lynn's door where I'm now caretaking.[45]
Jennifer Esson and Kara Leas, 16,
tied naked to trees in the woods east of Newport
on the road over the mountains to Corvallis
waver through the air.
Tortured and strangled, found by loggers

two and a half weeks after they disappeared
from Moolack Beach
that year my mother and I lived in Waldport
and you and I met. Five years ago.

And Sheila Swanson and Melissa Sanders
teenagers too, tied naked to trees in the same woods
two and a half years before,
tortured and strangled,
found by hunters five months after they disappeared.
Though almost identical, neither case has ever been solved
though linked in questionable ways by early DNA tests
to the serial rapist killer, Bobby Jack Fowler
arrested in Newport six months after Jennifer and Kara[46]

and that guy walking me back 2 a.m.
from dancing at the Bay Haven
up the steep bluff to Lynn's house.
She's in Paris and I'm deep in remembering, writing
the memoir of my father's rape and ongoing sexual abuse of me.

He follows me out of the Bay Haven, he will accompany me home.
I love walking nights, towns like this after dancing, past the houses of the
          sleeping.
I love the dark, the stars, the season, the land and place. My body walking out

it's great dance energy. I love the freedom, I know the danger, I know
to protect myself. We walk up over Yaquina Bay.

I knew him six years ago on the dance floor in Florence
living on his boat on the Siuslaw.
Johnny and I danced
and he watched us from the bar, probably
one who assumed we were dealing coke
after my sister spread that rumor.

He was interesting, though not in a romantic way. Not sexually. Good
looking in the demanded ways, actually pretty to my eyes
in a Southern, familiar way, maybe
he was French, from New Orleans,
a female face in motion much of the time. A Vietnam Vet.

Now he's living here, moved his boat up. Getting around
Cape Perpetua was not easy, a storm came up, it took three days.
He begins to frighten me. His manner, something, feels off,
I didn't feel this of him in Florence although there was always something.
He invites me to his motel room to take a hot tub with him, that big place
on the Bay where next Christmas Christian Longo
will drown his wife and three small children.[47]
He rents there regularly
when he needs to get off the boat. He says
there'll be a couple of other guys there too.

> Christian Longo strangled his wife, Mary Jane
> and two year old daughter, Madison,
> stuffed them in suitcases, dropped them into the Yaquina.
> He dropped Zachery and Sadie off a bridge into the Alsea at
>   Waldport
> with rocks tied around their ankles.

> He says now from death row
> he didn't believe
> he was the guy who did what he was convicted of.[48]
> He believed he was innocent.
> Then the psychiatrist explained to him
> the narcissistic personality disorder called Compensatory,

basically self-centeredness related to a damaged core sense of self
and Disassociation, the inability to acknowledge such of oneself.

"I dream a few times a week about my daughters, they're happy
and playing, it's pleasant. But my mind, even in the dream, knows
the reality. And it always switches
to an image of my son, Zachery, that haunts me
for the rest of the dream state."

Now this man walking me up the Newport bluff is talking about
the naked dead girls tied to the trees on 20
that no one else will talk about, saying
he knows who did it. A guy

helped him to sail up from Florence.
There was a big storm, took three days.
All they had was whiskey, they thought they were goners.
The guy confessed he was the killer.

Where is he now? I ask.
Inland, near Corvallis.
And told the story again of the three day voyage around Cape Perpetua,
a tone of shock, dismay, bewilderment.
And about those two earlier girls tied to trees, that case never solved either,
the first I've heard anyone mention those murders. Four local girls
kidnapped, tortured, strangled, murdered.
Not even Lynn remembers. *NO!* she'll exclaim
as if offended that I ask.
I walk us right past her street, up
to the main drag, 101, and somehow
get free of him. But from that night I'm frightened
he'll figure out
where I am.

He claimed to know the killer
but I didn't consider calling the police
        (I didn't want my father arrested.
He seemed slightly delirious. He wasn't drunk. It was something else.

I learned in childhood to never tell anyone
for fear of the courts, their foster homes with awaiting men.
And to not make my mother an orphan again
the legal immoral Court
and penal system.

I didn't believe him.

"Often times, the victim will try to repeat
the experience in later life, inviting repetition."
Neil Goldschmidt explained Elizabeth Dunham
supposedly putting herself in danger of being raped again.
"Bobby Jack Fowler believed that women he came in contact with
hitchhiking or in bars wanted to be sexually assaulted."
Could this guy have thought that about me?"

Do I put myself in such danger, am I inviting repetition
dancing in the Bay Haven Tavern, then walking home 2 a.m. alone?
Am I wanting to be raped again?
NO!
But this
will be deduced. Is my vision of love
gullibleness? A serious distortion? Disassociation? Is
Jesus'? The Goddess' before him

        if
        you invite the repetition
        it is to test the denied
                (it did happen

        to understand
        the Mystery at the core of your being
        the Mystery denied, never acknowledged, looked at
        believed
        comprehended

        to know yourself
        to go there again to grasp it
        to know what was done to you
        to break through the denial

their deepest hypnosis, your own,
to remind yourself

the poet's Negative Capability

the moral path not to see in black and white
either/or
the spiritual effort to find a way
of turning the other cheek
a way that moves us forward,
of not turning on the sadomasochistic wheel

to test Love, to love thy enemy as thyself
to know your enemy is temporarily insane
as in Aikido, the Japanese spiritual practice
of defending the self while at the same time
protecting the attacker from injury
in his temporary insanity

to find freedom as a woman
to fold not to the fear
to follow not men's rules for women,
inverting the mother and son to the son and the mother
patriarchy's universal laws for controlling women
that make you victim in the first place

to not let him enforce the blackmail
the veil

to claim your one and only life
the sacredness of the self
to live deliberately, and not
when you come to die, discover
you have not lived

to go out to the Mystery (there are many)
rather than hide from it

not wanting it again, but not letting the fear
control you, limit your life

> *staying in uncertainty*
> *innocent until proven guilty*
> *beyond a shadow of doubt*
>
> *"I will not give you the power*
> *to make me hate…"*[49]

That's when you knock on my door.
We stand in Lynn's living room.
You tell me of your fall from your company's scaffold
on the Bay Front, the surgery on your head.
"Don't cut my hair," you managed unconscious from the table.
"Don't cut his hair!" the nurses cried.
And they didn't. That's the awe
and respect you elicit, the distilled dignity
you retain, our not being racist
your possession of yourself

But you seem troubled, strained.
I assume it's the fall.

I give you my new book of poetry
with the Alima Prayer poems you inspired.
"Her strange incantations, litanies and tongues…" a critic writes.
"Her germinal codes…respect for all species, her fusion
of international and accidental events, ritual, praise for the body, human
commitment and reconciliation."[50]
You explain you felt like a substitute for Ramon
my first story. Jennifer

Kara, Sheila and Melissa
tied to trees thrum around us. I suddenly know
what's missing in my poems

Screaming   Sobbing   Tears

> *down the face, down the naked body*
> *I myself can't bear to look at*
> *but exposed here for all the world to find*
> *that will not know the sorrow*
> *the shame, the shock, the horror, these tears*

crying for my mother
she who would not recognize me now
this awkward new body
newly sprouted in breasts and hair and blood

but body he so covets
his lust for what you hate
the fear of it you live with
this stripping you naked to see
and possess, his torture
that makes him so happy
your tears he so loves
This most common act down through time
This most unacknowledged crime

except in becoming one with the killer
by killing him

this tied naked to the tree
freezing, reliving
your stupid little mistake, just
getting into his truck
to prove
you don't mistrust him

as you watch him tie and strangle your best friend   naked
as you are made witness to her struggle and cries   naked
as you struggle not to know   naked
you're next   naked
or the headlines

your tears
making the sky shine blue
making the grass grow green

Those girls wavering here, dear Man, dear Love at the door
does not mean I suspect you

or that you are guilty of Beth. It's just the fear. Just everything.
Paranoia of my boundless compassion, my vow
never to lose it. My proving
I don't mistrust you.
But in this writing I learn of myself
I remember my father
I realize about my mother
culture's silence and denial
my sister, our girls not mourned
all the girls every day down through time
every day of my girlhood, a girl dead in the paper
stuffed in trash cans, car trunks, dumped along the LA River

and boys too
but not reported in the papers

You are innocent until proven guilty
beyond a shadow of doubt, this writing
is simply the logics
of any patterning, any such wheel
and the sacred responsibility to think
of everything
crying here nailed naked to the tree

       But Love, if you are guilty
       again, I stay by you.

          (We are ovulating against us

these men who regularly down through history
rape and murder women

Who are these men, who
their victims?

       Why?
            *

10. Megan

The murder of Megan Kanka occurred on July 29, 1994 in Hamilton Township, Mercer Country, New Jersey. She was seven when she was raped and murdered by her neighbor Jesse Timmendequas, born April 15, 1961, who had two previous convictions for sexually assaulting young girls (a five year old and a seven year old).

He lures you into his house across the street
"Come see my puppy, oh, you will love him!"

He rams his thing into you.
You sink your new front teeth
into his hand, though you know not
what he's doing
slicing you in two, dividing
what wasn't divided
to make you
him

He slams you onto the dresser.
You can't breathe, it hurts beyond any hurt ever known.

> *Seven too, I thought*
> *when he kills us then*
> *it's sex too, part*
> *of the thrill*

At the trial Jesse's brother testified
hearing him screaming as their father raped him
nightly. But *rape*
in my 1984 Webster's New World Dictionary
is defined:
"the crime of having sexual intercourse with a woman or a girl
forcibly and without her consent."

He moves your body to his truck. Dead,
he rapes you again, the arousal
of his creation, o passive child
of his fantasies
              o possession mine

> *the deep mystical satisfaction*
> *we know in murder*
> *In going to war*
>
> *"After awhile murder is not just a crime of lust or violence.*
> *It becomes possession. They become*
> *a part of you, you two*
> *are forever one. And the grounds*
> *where you kill them or leave them*
> *become sacred to you.*
> *You will always be drawn back to them.*
> *I repeatedly returned to Sarah, dug her up*
> *and made love to her*
> *until putrefaction became too great.*
> *I decapitated twelve of my girls with a hacksaw*
> *kept their heads in my apartment. In Utah I applied*
> *make-up to Melisa Smith's face*
> *and washed Laura Anne's hair every day.*
> *It's like being God."*[51]

before placing you, Megan, in your wooden toy chest
and dumping you in Mercer County Park

The next day he confesses, leads
the police to the site

bloodstains, hair, and fiber samples, the bite mark
on his hand, your teeth

"I believe he is exactly the kind of predator," the Congressman screams
one with your rapist-killer
"that the legislature had in mind
when it enacted the death penalty."

One month later, New Jersey passes
Megan's Law
that requires sex offender registration,
community notification of registered sex offenders
and life in prison for repeat sex offenders.

Three months later, in November, Oregon
overwhelmingly voted for
Measure 11

> *-No possibility of probation*
> *-The sentencing judge cannot give a lesser sentence than prescribed by Measure 11*
> *nor can a prisoner's sentence be reduced for good behavior*
> *-Prisoners cannot be paroled prior to serving their minimum sentence*
> *-All 15 year olds and over tried as adults*
> *-Violent criminals cannot be reformed through probation or short prison sentences.*
> *The time they are kept incarcerated is itself a benefit to society*

Dear Megan, oh little girl
that you were prevented
from living your life. The sorrow
that you'll never be again

that such killers, so common,
mothers' sons,
who have no concept of the other, only of themselves
the pain they inflict
nailing us to the tree

Is this what you gave your life for?
Little Megan, this Law in your name?
Are we using you too?

*

11. The Truth, The Whole Truth, Nothing But The Truth As I Promised You

"Ask any experienced defense lawyer: the real risks are for an accused person who is innocent. A guilty defendant has many more options available." The New York Times

Dear Sharon, December 23, 2006, TRCI, Umatilla, Oregon

"On September 24, 2004 I was found guilty of sexual abuse on three charges. One, for which I received one hundred months, and two others, for which I received seventy-five months on each. Since one of the 75 month allegations was part of the same act as the 100 months sentence, Judge Branford had the 75 months to run concurrent so I received 175 months.

The first, I'm accused of inserting my finger into Beth's vagina. The other two are for hovering, caressing her breasts.

There was another incident which equaled the above charge, but Beth's story had changed so much, the judge threw it out. She had claimed I had come into her bedroom, she didn't know where from, and had started caressing her, had uncovered her, pulled up her nightie, and ran my hands over her breasts, eventually moved down to her panties and eventually pushed them down enough to insert my finger into her. She claimed in the report given to the officer from California, that I knelt down by her bed, and after I got into her panties, I masturbated. All had taken 45 minutes. She stated that she was paralyzed by fear and did nothing. At the trial she said I sat on her bed and caressed her thigh for about 5 minutes.

Another incident occurred, allegedly at the same apartment you came to. Beth and her mom, named Teanne, would come over and spend one night or several. One night Teanne and I went out, Beth stayed at the place, with my son Graham. She slept on the couch. She claimed that I came in after her mom had, and did the same thing as the above, this time lasting 30 minutes.

That night I did come in behind Teanne, because she smoked in the car and I wanted to cool down, overheated by dance, and get some fresh air. I came upstairs, got a drink of water, looked into my bedroom, went to the bathroom and then to bed. Teanne's testimony is the same as mine. It should have been thrown out then. (Time lapse out of car to bed, about fifteen minutes.)

About the only time anything at all could have happened, we three talk about at different times. One night at the same apartment, Graham had some friends over to spend the night, so Beth came to bed with Teanne and myself.

At some point, Teanne, sleeping in the middle, got up to use the bathroom. While she was gone I rolled over thinking Beth was her and touched her shoulder, realized it was not Teanne. I rolled back.

Beth claims that the same thing happened as in the first two incidents.

Now the trouble starts. About two days later Teanne asked me whether or not anything had happened, at all. I lied and say no, because I don't want her to think I would harm Beth in any way.

All this was supposed to have happened between January 1, of 95 and Dec 31, of 96.

Beth and her mom move to California and when she was in high school her class was asked to write their autobiography and share with the class or share one-to-one with the teacher. Beth chose the latter. In the assignment she wrote that living in Oregon was difficult and the teacher wanted to know what made it hard. Beth mentions a few things and includes that I had touched her.

The teacher calls the LA police (as required by law) and they take a statement at school claiming the two incidents in which I supposedly caress her, get into her panties and insert my finger. Later the officer takes her home and Beth explains to her mom what was happening.

During that interview they both recall the incident when she was in bed with us and Teanne used the bathroom, adding that I had done the same as before and when her mom returned I quickly roll over and pretend to sleep.

She claims all of this to happen in fewer than five minutes but says nothing, as in the other two times she said she didn't know what was happening and never tried to stop it. She also said she could hear her mom coming down the hall; the bedroom and bath doors are back to back. There is no hall.

I met Teanne in '91. My brother Garry had just passed. Bob, Teanne's husband, was dying in much the same way, due to their involvement with the military. I spent months with my beloved Garry at the end. He was everything to me. While I was there, I saw unconditional love given to him by his wife Deborah. The compassion I have I shared with Bob, and we became friends, and visited often.

Again, I saw the love between Teanne and Bob as in Garry and Deborah. It was something I had not experienced. Soon Bob passed.

The love between Garry and myself I cherish till my last breath. As I have told you before he raised me in and out of the school. That love I know.

I feel that same love exists between Beth and her mom.

I learn that Trish Miller, a county detective, receives a report of the allegations and finds me. I tell her that the only time anything at all could have happened was the time Beth had shared my bed with her mom. Now what? I ask. She suggests the polygraph test. I agree and three days later when her boss is available we spend three hours together and I pass the poly twice, again mentioning the shared bed incident. I was asked if I had ever touched Beth's breasts or vagina.

They tell me I am free to go. I ask what to expect. Miller said it takes about two weeks for the grand jury to decide if there is enough to press charges. I wait two and a half months.

All this time Miller is aware that I was on my way to Canada. I told her where I was going to go, how to reach me by phone or mail and I would return if I had to.

About a year and a half later I get the warrant in the mail. I was unaware of the two incidents of penetration, am shocked, so I call Miller. I told her I would return and as it was, I got arrested at the border and spend six months in the Lincoln County Jail.

Here's the sticker. After the polygraphs I'm concerned about Beth and what might have happened in California. I ask if I could send a note through Miller to Beth and express my concern. She said she would send it. It is Friday, I'm drinking heavy, tequila, alone the entire weekend, as I had done too much of at that time.

Naturally my plans to leave and concern for Beth are fixed in my mind. On Sunday I wrote to her, intoxicated, and depressed. First I write about my concern, that something awful might have occurred in California, then tell her of the polygraph and that I didn't know what would be, but that I had told the truth.

I write about her relationship with her mom and compare it with Garry and myself, and I felt responsible if any breakdown had occurred between them, because I had lied to her mom of the shoulder incident, I quickly knew she was not Teanne, her hair is long, to her mid back and curly, like yours. Beth's is short and straight.

I never ever wanted anything to cause a breakdown between Garry and me. In fact I would tell him only enough to protect him.

I'm drunk remembering.

I start to apologize and go overboard with it. My spelling and everything about that letter is bad. (Even worse than this.) My handwriting is usually pretty good and easy to read, maybe even neat! I give the letter to Trish Miller, early Monday morning. She said she would make sure Beth got it. I feel good about that. I included two small eagle feathers from the underside of the left wing.

Instead of mailing the letter Miller opens it and the charges are built out of the apology for that little lie to Teanne.

Well, over one and a half years later I am arrested. The rest you know, at least I think so. If you want to know more let me know.

"The truth and nothing but" includes: I love you. Jack.

P.S. The poly is not admissible in court. The part about that and about the truth was omitted from what the jury was able to see.

There were many Newport character witnesses. No one had a single negative thing to say against me. Beth took back everything on the stand. Teanne said "I can say nothing, nothing, not one bad thing against Jack Retasket."

*

12. Cross Examination: The Truth, The Whole Truth, Nothing But The Truth As We Promised Each Other

I'm accused of inserting my finger into Beth's vagina.
Of hovering, caressing her breasts.

You don't deny this, you just report their charges.
Not the whole truth but a way to keep your new promise to me
not to lie

And another incident
but Beth's story had changed so much
the judge threw it out.

Why does this sound like you're casting aspersions
on Beth's character?

Another incident occurred, allegedly at the same apartment you came to.

Allegedly. Did it or did it not? This would be
the couch we sat on
where she slept
beneath the array of eagle feathers.

….got a drink of water, looked into my bedroom, went to the bathroom and then to bed.

This seems to indicate that the bathroom had two entrances, one
not from the bedroom. From a hall?

There is no hall.

She had claimed I had come into her bedroom….

Where was this bedroom? Siletz? Cobb Mountain?
Claimed? Did you or did you not?

All this was supposed to have happened
between January 1 of 95 and December 31 of 96.

Did it? Were you deep in sexual obsession and violation
of the daughter of your lover when you met me?
Almost a year into it? None of this I intuited.
Could you have been hoping I might save you
from the "trap" of them?

The daughter of your lover.... Why
are men so universally, so perversely, unfaithful?
Do you teach each other
this is the way to be a man?

Nowhere do you tell the whole truth. But of course
this is written for your jailers too.

Beth mentioned a few things
and included that I had touched her.

What few things?
Did you touch her?

The teacher calls the LA Police.
They take a statement at school claiming the two incidents
in which I supposedly caress her, get into her panties and insert my finger.

Supposedly?

I rolled over thinking Beth was Teanne
and touched her shoulder, realized it was not Teanne.
I rolled back.

But this touching was so disturbing to Beth
she told her mother almost immediately.

About two days later Teanne asked me whether or not anything had happened, at all.
I lied and say no, because I don't want her to think I would harm Beth in any way.

You did harm her. Did you not know this?

She stated that she was paralyzed by fear, and did nothing....

Did you imagine that because she did nothing she liked it?
Her doing nothing signified to you to continue? To lead the way?
Did you believe this was your male role? To harm her?
Was this before our gig at the Paris Theater in Portland, or after?
Teanne in our audience?
Was she checking on you?

> *oh tell me Soul*
> *of Teanne, the mother*

I quickly knew it was not Teanne, her hair is long
to her mid back and curly, like yours.
Beth's is short and straight.

There's the phenomenon
of sleep rapists. Like sleep walkers
they can't be held accountable. Are you
feigning sleep innocence?

I believed what you told me earlier.
When Beth got home with the officer to her mother
she took it all back, she was writing fiction.
Or did I make that up? My Creative Writing aesthetics
(against fiction), my
soul path

I believed what you told me
but I would have supported you
if guilty

…. and insert my finger into her

The word would be ram, jam, stab, stick, force, plunge.
Insert implies gentleness, carefulness, almost
foreplay as in sexy, as in erotic   as in sanitary
the hygienic tampon.
It would have been fast, given Teanne in the bathroom
just beyond the wall, back to back: *there is no hall.*
It would have been force
It would have been rape

Was the finger insertion a repeat
of what you did
when you were the thirteen year old baby sitter
with the ten year old Sharon?
The delicious secret between you, just
kids?

I met Teanne in '91

How old was Beth then?
Were you trying to get back into the family, to your twin sister
you shared inside your mother, your tribe
the Church and State destroyed?

Was Bob Beth's father? Who
was Beth's father?

She said she could hear her mom coming down the hall.
There is no hall.

Nothing she says is reliable.
Nothing allows her fear, her cry for her mother
Your role, Pluto, to take the daughter from the mother
the awkward new woman crying for her mother
as you the son were taken, as she the mother
was taken

so now you take

(You want back in, this
is incest

I learn that Trish Miller
a county detective

just off the Christian Longo murder trial
still on that adrenalin rush, that international news

receives a report of the allegations and finds me.
I pass the poly twice mentioning the shared bed incident. I was asked
if I had ever touched Beth's breasts or vagina.

Did you ever touch Beth's breasts or vagina?

Was the report of allegations before or after
you knocked on my door in Newport,
the last time I saw you?
Is this why you seemed troubled, strained?
Were you already in deep trouble?
Is this why you fled to Canada?

After the polygraphs I'm concerned about Beth
and what might have happened in California.

Something must have happened to her in California
to cause her to falsely accuse you.
Someone else to blame for her blaming you
        (Was this twisting her not harmful to her?)
        Were you only in lust with her?

About a year and a half later I get the warrant in the mail.

They were waiting for Measure 11 to become the law
before they nabbed you.

I was unaware of the two incidents of penetration, am shocked
so I call Miller. I told her I would return.
You'd a thought I was a terrorist the way they handled me at the border.

I was shocked too, the front page.
"The foreign object was just his finger!" I gasped to others
revealing my own warped state, a finger to me
is not a foreign object.
"He admits lusting for her." This was your honesty,
believability, my generosity and wisdom. Don't all guys
lust after virgin girls? Isn't this natural? My
father

Of the Fifteen Minimum Sentences mandated by Measure 11
seven are sexual violations.[52]
"Penetration by a foreign object"
is Measure 11 wording

Is this the Christian Longo Syndrome?
You can't believe you could have done what you were found guilty of?
Are you innocent? (Do you believe
you are innocent? Is this disassociation? Does your mind in deepest
           dream
know exactly what you've done? As it knew who and what caused this
as you plummeted yourself down
to the Oblate's face on the prison cell floor?

Did you imagine that she liked it? What does a male
segregated from females all his life, from his mother, his twin sister
know? Were you instructed
this was your male role, your male responsibility?

Sometimes I still hear
the most preposterous gender notions

           Bobby Jack Fowler believed
             women want to be sexually assaulted.

How would you know how to love a woman?
How would you know how to love me
from all your male prisons?

little boy kidnapped from his family, twin sister and tribe
your heart imprisoned. What would you know of the other sex?
How would you know how to love
except to revert back to age five?

I never ever wanted anything to cause a breakdown between Garry and me.
In fact I would tell him only enough to protect him.

           But somewhere in your letters you tell
           that Garry always blamed you
           for what he was guilty of

           as my father and mother and sister
           blamed me for that which they were guilty.
           I couldn't know this. What I could know and do

was to love them more.
                    (Is this sadomasochism?)

And hey, Garry was your elder! Who's protecting who,
and what is being protected?

To you lying is loving.
You learned this from the Church.
You learned this from the State.
You grew your secret self.
You save your soul, you masturbate

little runaway hiding in the apple pickers' cabins
with your box of light.
To tell the truth is to bring the Law down
To tell the truth is to bring God down
on you

I start to apologize, go overboard.
That letter was clearly written by an inebriated person.
This should have been noted in the trial

I give the letter to Trish Miller

whose dishonesty, lying, betrayal, trickery
is legal, honorable, is the Law. Our respect for this.
Our money and fame. Our legal system

          our lost little boy
          raped by the Oblate
          sticking his nail in the light switch
          to kill himself

          our lost little boy
          inserting his finger
          into the box of light
          of his first love, age ten

You've loved her silence and stillness
ever since your complete fantasy

your safe home, your one sacred place, your solace

to make her female (this was irresistible) (your delicious job)
to find your twin sister and mother
to claim yourself at last
to redeem the Oblate who took possession
of you for eternity at seven
to comprehend how and why
he could have done that to you, man
of God
          everyman who put you here

to redeem your raped parents
all your raped people

your father
in Kamloops Residential School too
at the loss of his father
        (what happened to your grandfather?)
        all your grandfathers, the warriors

Crazy Horse   Sitting Bull

all your grandmothers, their children
        their vulvas scalped

worn on the hats of the soldiers
parading in the ranks

on your land

What did Crazy Horse sexually fantasize
after finding the young sister of Long Spear
at the Sand Creek Massacre
"scalped in a bad place"?[53]

*

I include two small eagle feathers from the underside of the left wing

13. Irresistible

a.

"Do you deal with *why*?" a man sighed
after my first reading from my father book.
Only later, flying down the freeway
did I catch his meaning
only later   only now

the unspoken question
        the accusation
all my life
always dismissed, never answered

        how could I
        answer that?

the secret, deepest response of many
even now, their

        resentment   their
        inside-out
        compliment   their
        blame

            In infancy, at seven
            I was irresistible

                    oh, boy, aren't I the lucky one
                    to make him feel like a man
                    to be desired
                    to make her jealous

                    lucky me, myth
                    of the irresistible   taboo
                    of acknowledging it

                    my sister jealous
                    she wasn't irresistible
                    to our helpless father

> our mother's disbelief
> "You didn't know
> you were beautiful?"

> Mama, their staring
> made me ugly

What was I to do with their making me
irresistible? What are we
to do with his *why*? His
rhetorical question, his unspoken answer, his all-knowing
silence, his wisdom, his sexy lust, his

> masculinity, really
> we all know
> the reason for his common crime
> since the beginning of time

What was my mother to do? All Greece
hated Helen, could love her only when she was laid
white ash amid funeral cypresses. We all know why
this most common crime
since the beginning of time
the rape of Helen, the beginning of Western Civilization, not,
dear first poet, H.D., God's daughter born of love

Irresistible.
Psyche carries the secret of life from the Underground, Persephone's
beauty secret sealed in a coffin.
Chief Sweetwater's Box of Light, Darwin's
Theory of Evolution

the Tennessee monkey trial my father attended as a boy
with his mother, poet, reporter, and Baptist, witnessed
the famous dueling attorneys, William Jennings Bryan[54]
and for the defense, Clarence Darrow
his hero for the rest of his life

> whose ridicule of his mother's Christianity
> with Darwin's theory of natural selection

"affected him deeply. Dog eat dog,"
my mother lectured, *"the survival of the fittest.*
The human race owes its survival
to its lower instincts."

In Mine City Baptist Church afterwards
every Sunday singing *Amazing Grace*
a boy, the last child at home
beside his beloved mother
instructing him in the higher instincts, slowly
he understands
he can't be like her, he must
wrench himself from her
a wretch like him
to be a man
he must be
like his father
embrace his lower instincts
which give him
so much pleasure anyway
explains, excuses, redeems his cruel unfathomable father

"the terrible things that went on in that house"

Diana caught Actaeon accidentally at her bath
set his own dogs on him. Metaphor
for masturbation, *dog eat dog*
image of her he stole
for his future fantasies, the Church
labeled sin to control.
She wore his head as her crown. Never me

such vengeance, his head
to proclaim the Unforgivable.
Not me, not ever. Forgive him, World
he knows not what he does. Is this
my mistake?

Peeping Tom struck blind
was Godiva's punishment. Still in diapers

I protested. Hate the sin, not
the sinner, I didn't hate my father.
I didn't want him blinded or in shackles, eaten
by his own dogs or fellow man, crucified, beheaded
in Hell for Eternity.
In the crib I knew the suck of sadomasochism, almost
irresistible. I would not become
what I hate. They laughed
I was just having
a fit.

Irresistible?
We are born without control of our body eliminations.
Then, our universal success.
Behold all over the world, all cultures

my body, Godiva's like Jesus'
Behold! and gave her only begotten self to the world
that we might live. Political, our bodies through time

What haven't I done
to deal with why, what haven't I pled, allowed
loved, denied, embraced, forsaken
to tell the sin of the beholders? To forgive
but not forget their crime against us, boys and girls, men and women.
Life.
To evolve it   To ovulate against us

b. *To Scar the Newborn Boy*
> *"…at the bris*
> *of brokenness"*[55]

"A man's images, fantasies
is his superiority, his evolution from the woman
who remains in the body," my great male poet
informed my daughter and me. "This is the reason
for the Bris, the Kabbala's instructions
to send the eight day old male in pain and betrayal
up into the mind away from the body
away from her
in order to create

the abstract, the
alphabet"[56]

the jealous Fathers' decree
to make the mother the male's betrayer.
To claim the boy just out of her body
on whom he feeds, but with this cut
can never now trust.

c.   *Why Are Men Sexually Attracted to Children?*

The passivity of those in his mind
created nightly in his fantasy.
Children he creates
all by himself. Children
in his complete control

Superior   Master   God   Child
he is   his privacy
we guard as sacred

his vulnerability, deep fragility
our sons, our brothers, our father, our lovers

and he hates us for this

d. *What Haven't I Done?*

I enter your cell, to try out irresistible
to understand
the man rising in me
at her, little daughter
lost sister, big girl
I can't help myself   I let go
      to the dark blue tunnel of eternity, the light, electrical
      in the box, my
      self   my right
      my nature   the nature
      of my manhood
            my inalienable self
            my natural selection
            the survival of the fittest

I know irresistible
witnessed all my life

all the movies rerunning
the boy school of literature
inside my lovers   the boy father
I came out of

my manhood
requiring this
to lead the way
              (to take by force
your every breath, mine again, this is
necessary, this is duty, this is best for you
I spread you open   I insert myself   I enter the land

          the conquistadors to the natives
          the guard to the prisoner
          the general to the private
          the private to the enemy
          God to the Man
          the priest to the boy
          the parent to the child
          the boy to the girl
          the fathers at the witches
          the fathers at their sons

Why are such men
turned on by children?

               Because they were sexually abused
               as children

     she will circle the Mansion again
     he will go to jail again
     he will kill himself rather than know

the Oblate to the seven year old

         I'm understanding even
         the Oblate's lust

To stay in life. To affirm it happened
To know why you're crazy
To forgive the rapist
To understand   the soul
demanding justice, the reality inside
redeeming what was done to the sacred self

to claim the other as thy self
to penetrate the 8th grade mouth of Elizabeth
to touch the 11 year old thigh of Beth

to insert yourself, Daddy, into your 7 year old self

to claim your lover's child as yours
to be as physical as its mother

to touch her vagina again
your twin sister emerging with you at the door[57]
to the light from which you entered in the beginning
the orgasmic light of your father
to your mother, the orgasmic light
of your mother receiving him
the orgasmic light of your parents
creating you

                then (screaming three days until she dies
                you and all the younger ones in the next room
                your father falling apart   life
                and death
                the orgasmic light

to know the denied
to reclaim the denied

the man rising   the fittest
to overcome
the mother's supremacy

the father's necessity
the Law's authority
the Other's reality
the fact of you
irresistible
I can't help myself   the birth wave that propels me
out of her
                    your self no one knows

I press that self into you
myself no one knows
I press myself into you again

to love you as myself
to make you me

to find myself again
my secret sacred self
I put my finger in

                e.
What haven't we done
to know why? What haven't we begged, prayed, allowed
denied, embraced, forsaken, forgiven, fantasized? Murdered. Grown back
our foreskin, grown back our hymen. Turned water into wine
bread into blood   heaven
into wages

What haven't we claimed
What haven't we given up
to tell the sin of the beholders? To
inform them. To
evolve it

God's child still born
of rape

not love
                         *

I begin with your name, Kha-che-chee, and that horse
at the water of your painting, forehead soaking as it drinks, until it
disappears
and the water mirrors the sky, the stars and the moon

14. Time

"Forgiveness and justice are not mutually exclusive and compassion is a subversive act."
Paul Fericano[58]

"Only love is holy, and love's ecstasies." H.D.

You say with tears
from the box of light
I love you
for wanting to protect your father
when he molested you. You say
from the box of light
thank you

> They will say I'm empowering you
> They will say this is blindness
> the victim's complicity, irresistible, that hypnosis
> > to repeat
> > the evil done to the self
> > by doing it to others
>
> > to another child
>
> > and what are we going to do
> > with the psychopaths?

> They will say Love
> is sickness. How
> can I be sitting here?

> How can I not be sitting here?
> Face to face, you and I
> Love

We are ordered to rise from our seats
line up against the far wall
women and children

Then each of you
our fathers, brothers, husbands, sons,
last names called out

males the imprisoned, females the visitors
one at a time, from the seat we left you in

line up at the opposite door you came through
until we are twin lines across the room
obedient boys and girls of kindergarten
our eyes across the light and hush
of empty chairs
to each other. Everyone
trying to take away
all that can be seen.

You are the last to be called
sitting alone with your cane in the furthest corner
your eyes cast down
in the hush
our eyes in the hush on you
mine. I feel the pain you try to hide
to stand up straight and warrior proud
Crazy Horse when he surrenders
coming in to their Reservation

Then north across the rivers, back to Walla Walla, this once holy site, the radio
on my rental car

> *"Today one of the highest officials of the Church*
> *was arrested in Phoenix*
> *the vicar general of the Roman Catholic Diocese*
> *on charges he fondled boys and young men*
> *and asked them prying questions about their sex lives*
> *as part of confession."*

At Wallulu, where the Walla Walla
enters the Columbia
the marker tells of Wih-mun-ke-wakan, Walks Far Woman
an Iowa Indian, also known as La Guivoise, Marie Dorion
and *Aiaouez,* later rendered as *Iowa,*
the second known woman, after Sacagawea
to come west overland.[59] She hid the winter of 1811-12
in the Blue Mountains, the winter of the earthquake

that caused the Mississippi to flow backwards for five days
with her two young boys, "probably two and four,"
after their father and the other white men
of the Wilson Price Hunt Party of the Pacific Fur Company
were killed by the Bannock.

Aiaouez knew how to survive
the cold and starvation, the unknown wilderness,
how to get her boys to safety in the spring.

> How many feet deep, Kha-che-chee, did you say
> is the cement so you can't dig out?
> here where the Snake, the Walla Walla, the Umatilla
> together turn the south-flowing Columbia
> west I hear her keening

> *don't let them ever find us*

I will be big as love for you I will be wise enough O World
whirling backwards, dangerous
and endangered. I will turn
the rivers   I will dream
through volcanic rock
a hideout for you on the coast

big as Crazy Horse's parents who removed him from the scaffold
and carried him away, burying him
in a place we cannot find

big as Rachel Carson
whose work to limit DDT
on the Modoc's captured land
enabled the endangered bald eagle to revive
though she herself was dying of cancer

big as your father at Kamloops Residential School
tongue bleeding from the steel embedded strap
when he uttered his language
but when he finished Kamloops
he knew English

while keeping his five-year-old secret vow
to carry his native language back
to the people

       I am innocent, we
       are innocent   Teanne and Beth are innocent
       All.
       I would repeat what I did with my father at seven
       I would not tell, I would not hand him over
       to the State, to
       further evil

       though I forever reel too
       and vow to keep pushing
       from our vastly destroyed hearts
       to address the oldest sin

       abuse of

       my twin
       our twin

       our soulmate
       you, myself

       body of all ourselves

       our little boys

              our little girls

       hidden in the ruins

            You hold the Box of Light in your hands, Neil Goldschmidt

            As you do, Kha-che-chee
            As you do, Wih-mun-ke-wakan, Aiaouez, Iowa.
            As you do Waldport White

            As you do, Michael Dorris

As you do, Father

Amnesty is forgiveness, not
forgetting

*

(April 17, 2005-January 2015
Two Rivers Correctional Institution, Umatilla, Oregon-
Mendocino, California)

1 But I failed in the initial petition of Neil Goldschmidt. There are complex reasons for my failure, but my old fidelity to my family, my knowing well the collective psychic refusals to deal with this common crime, being intimidated by the poetic task, and, no doubt, by the fear and apprehension of my inevitable blindnesses are some of them.

2 And there is the aesthetic issue, the booklength poem here feels unpoetic, too prose-y. (Some of the most poetic pieces I've written in this long investigative process do not fit into the overall fourteen-part structure, not even as free-standing poems.) All along I've regretted not having cast "The Visit" as prose, which would have been a far easier task, and probably more effective. I suppose my love and belief in the political and spiritual value of poetry could not be abandoned.

3 "Crazy Horse was born to parents from two tribes of the Lakota division of the Sioux, his father was an Oglala and his mother was a Miniconjou." Crazy Horse, Wikipedia, p. 2.

4 "Wyoming," *Hard Country,* Sharon Doubiago. 1982, 1999, p. 141.

5 *Investigative Poetry*, City Lights, 1976, and a special pdf reprint published by Blake Route Press, Woodstock, NY.

6 University of Pittsburgh, 1992, p. 1.

7 The Anderson Valley Advertiser, November 20, 2013.

8 *A Broken Life,* p. 3, http://www.salon.com/1997/04/21/dorris/

9 Doubiago, *The Husband Arcane.   The Arcane of O*, Performance Poets Series, Gorda Plate Press, a division of *New Settler Interview,* Mendocino, California. 1996.

10 Neil Goldschmidt, born June 16, 1940; Mayor of Portland, Oregon: 1973-79; U.S. Secretary of Transportation: 1979-81; Governor of Oregon: 1987-91.

11 The statement was issued on Neil Goldschmidt's behalf by the Portland firm Gard and Gerber, May 7, 2004.

12 Goldschmidt's portrait was removed from the state capitol. On February 1, 2011 (two weeks after Elizabeth Dunham's death at the age of forty nine and her name was released to the press), he published the following public statement in the *Oregonian: "In the 35 years since I failed this young woman, her family, and my family, the pain has never eased. There are days when I believe it would be better if I were lifted from this earth and removed as a cause of pain for others and to find quiet for myself. Until this occurs, I will do my best to remember the person I damaged by doing right by the lives that surround me. "* "In 2012 Goldschmidt was living in Portland and France in isolation and disgrace." Wayne Thompson, Oregon Encyclopedia, Oregon History and Culture.

13 "....or several months, according to Goldschmidt in his public confession, and for several years according to the victim." Wayne Thompson, Oregon Encyclopedia.

14 "The 30 Year Secret," Nigel Jaquiss, Willamette Week, May 12, 2004.

15 Margie Boulé, The Oregonian, February 1, 2011.

16 Rafael Yglesias, *Why I Chose to Work with Roman Polanski* – Slate, February 10, 2014
http://www.slate.com/articles/life/culturebox/2014/02/dylan_farrow_woody_allen_and_roman_polanski_why_i_chose_to_work_with_polanski.html.

17 Source lost. This is cited in earliest 2006 version of "The Visit" without source.

18 Goldschmidt, February 1, 2011.

19 The Snake enters the Columbia about 45 miles north of the Two Rivers Correctional Institution; the Walla Walla River enters about 30 miles north; from maps it appears that Two Rivers Correctional Institution is where the much smaller Umatilla River enters the Columbia from the south (the Umatilla is not on most maps). "What are the two rivers the prison is named for?" Jack thinks it is the Snake and the Columbia, as I long believed. The Columbia River makes an abrupt 90 degree turn west right there nearby somewhere.

20 Harper Collins, 1995.

21 Pregnancy chapter of *Son,* Sharon Doubiago (unpublished).

22 Gerald Vizenor, *Manifest Manners: Narratives of Postindian Survivance,* University of Nebraska Press, 1994. Vizenor accuses Dorris of pandering to white views of Native alcoholism after Dorris urged that alcoholic Native mothers be sent to prison.

23 *My Father's Love, Vol 2*, p. 354.

24 According to Google, Michael Dorris was featured at Seattle's Bumbershoot in both 1992 and 1993. I'm unsure from which year this memory stems.

25 "Keintpoos," is in both *Body and Soul* (2000) and *Love on the Streets* (2008), plus the following endnote explaining the Modoc Wars: "*Keintpoos is the Modoc chief more commonly known as Captain Jack. The Modoc Wars took place in the northeastern corner of California in 1873 along the Oregon-Applegate Trail. In a tragedy-ridden episode involving the demand for a statement of tribal solidarity due to looming genocide, Keintpoos killed General Canby at a peace conference, making Canby the only regular Army general killed in any Indian war. Keintpoos and three of his subchiefs were hanged at Fort Klamath, Oct 3, 1873, and the Modoc people sent as prisoners to northeastern Oklahoma, where most of them died. The few who survived were eventually returned to the Klamath Agency.*

Rachel Carson's Silent Spring *(Houghton Mifflin, 1962), generally acknowledged as the initiator of the modern environmental movement, tells the twentieth century story of the Modoc's land, the Tule River of California and the Upper Klamath Lake of Oregon: DDT from the surrounding reclamation lands drained into wildlife refuges, killing all life."*

[26] "Email To The End of the World," Sharon Doubiago, *Naked to the Earth* (unpublished).

[27] The North Thompson River—northern branch of the Thompson River, the largest tributary of the Frazer River—originates at the toe of the Thompson Glacier in the Premier Range of the Cariboo Mountains, west of the community of Valemount. The river flows generally south through the Shuswap Highlands of British Columbia.

[28] "The Retasket name is on the 1910 document of Sir Wilfrid Laurier," Prime Minister of Canada (1896-1911). "'Retasket' made it through the whole Indian residential school experience. It was probably because my family was a descendent of the hereditary chief. It came to me that Retasket is a Statlmx Indian word that means 'quick tempered.'" Mike Retasket Interview Transcript, by Dave Beckwith, http://comm-org.wisc.edu/papers2000/beckwith/retasket.htm. Mike Retasket, Bonaparte Band Council, Natural Resource Coordinator. Interview was 10/14/2000; found 9/13/2014.

[29] "Crazy Horse," *Hard Country,* Sharon Doubiago, West End Press, 1982, 1999, p.150.

[30] Priscilla (Ramos) Hunter, *Voices and Dreams,* 1991 (privately published by Bruce Levine). *"I belong to the Indian Shaker Church...."* The Indian Shaker Church is not related to the eastern European-American Shaker Church.

[31] The poem by Sir Isaac Newton was clipped from the local Waldport paper that week, Dec 2, 1995, and stapled to this letter.

[32] From the Paris Theater poster of the reading.

[33] The Raped Mute Syndrome: In Ovid's *Metamorphoses,* Tereus rapes Philomela and then cuts out her tongue so she cannot denounce him. But as with Maya Angelou, as with me, you go mute because to say anything is to betray something. Raped by her mother's lover, Maya's uncles murdered him, contributing to her trauma: *telling resulted in the murder of her mother's lover!*

[34] Letter from Jack Retasket, April 24, 2014.

[35] Jack Hirschman, "The Line of Light Arcane,"*#3. The Arcanes,* Multimedia Edizioni, Salerno, Italy, 2006, p. 467.

[36] The investigation into this Canadian genocide continues. "The probable site of this mass burial of the executed children has been located, is now under protection and jurisdiction of the Onkwehonwe Mohawk Nation and its clan mothers." *Mass Execution of Aboriginal Children of the Mohawk Residential School, Brantford, Ontario, 1943:* http://itccs.org/tag/brantford-mohawk-indian-residential-school/

[37] Wikipedia: "razor strop (or razor strap)."

[38] From the Oct 20, 2006 letter version of the rape, labeled the Second Version.

[39] In the Second Version he says "I would rather not use their names, the hate is toward Brother Shirley and all the robed bastards including the nuns." But in the October 9, 2014 phone call, he asked me if I remember these boys. He named them this time without reservations or requests.

[40] *"You own everything that happened to you. Tell your story. If people wanted you to write warmly about them they should have behaved better."* Ann Lamott, *Bird by Bird.*

[41] Henry David Thoreau, *Walden Pond.*

[42] May 1999. Publisher: Darkecho.com.

[43] July 6, 2004.

[44] William Ray, review of *My Father's Love, Vol. 2* (http://www.amazon.com/My-Fathers-Love-Vol-II/dp/0984130438/ref=pd_rhf_se_p_img_1).

[45] "I left Dec 24, 2000, for France. You came a few weeks later. I came back about June 2, 2001, and you drove to Portland to meet me." Lynn Jeffress.

[46] May 3, 1992: Sheila and Melissa Sanders, 17, disappeared from near Beverly Beach State Park where they had been camping. Their bodies were discovered October 10, 1992, east of Newport, up Highway 20, in a wooded area near Eddyville.

January 28, 1995, around 1 a.m., Jennifer Esson and Kara Leas, both 16, were last seen on NW 56th Street in Newport, Oregon, walking toward Highway 101, near Moolack Beach after leaving a friend's house. Their tortured and strangled bodies were discovered on February 15, 1995, by loggers in a wooded area, covered with brush, up Highway 20.

June 28, 1995, Bobby Jack Fowler met a woman in one of Newport's taverns. He imprisoned her in the Tides Inn. She jumped nude out the second floor window, a chain around her ankle. He was arrested by the Newport police. On January 18, 1996, he was given a 16 year sentence following a conviction for rape, kidnapping and attempted rape (*but not of the four previous murdered girls*). Bobby Jack Fowler died May 15, 2006, in Oregon State Prison in Salem Oregon, of lung cancer. There is much on the internet indicating police and informant foul play, would-be sex/killer fantasies and misinformation on Bobby Jack Fowler and the unsolved Oregon Coast murders.

[47] December 2001.

[48] "…I couldn't fathom the thought of being capable of doing what I was convicted of." Christian Longo http://www.kimatv.com/news/local/Words-of-a-Killer-Christian-Longo-writes-about-his-dead-family-165576656.html?tab=video&c=y.

[49] Martin Luther King, Jr.

---

[50] Joel Lipman, review of *Body and Soul*, The Temple, #18, ed by Charles Potts, Tsunami Press, Walla Walla, Washington, February 2001.

[51] This is Ted Bundy, serial rapist, killer, and necrophile, born Nov 24, 1946, Burlington Vermont. Both Bundy and the Green River Killer, Gary Leon Ridgway, born Feb 18, 1949, in Salt Lake City, Utah, often returned to the secret graves of their murdered women to disinter them and have sex with them. Ridgway wasn't apprehended until November 30, 2001. Ridgway is believed to have murdered at least 72 women near Seattle and Tacoma—"so many he lost count. Probably there are more." The majority occurred between 1982 and 1984. Many of the bodies were discarded on the Green River, south of Seattle, hence "The Green River Killer."

[52] 1st degree Rape, 2nd degree Rape, 1st degree Sodomy, 2nd degree Sodomy, 1st degree Unlawful sexual penetration, 2nd degree Unlawful sexual penetration, 1st degree Sexual abuse.
The rest are Manslaughter, Assault, Kidnapping and Robbery.

[53] "Wyoming," *Hard Country,* Sharon Doubiago. 1982, 1999, p. 141.

[54] William Jennings Bryan, b. May 19, 1860-d. July 26, 1925 in Dayton Tennessee (five days after the Scopes trial had ended). His response against the Theory of Evolution is poetic—linguistically impressive.

[55] *"The Line of Light Arcane,"* Jack Hirschman, *The Arcanes,* Multimedia Edizioni, 2006, Salerno, Italy. p. 500 of 447-502.

[56] "My Lovers' Mirrors," Sharon Doubiago, *Naked to the Earth* (unpublished).

[57] Wendy Retasket was born March 25, 1950, minutes after her twin brother, Jack. She died May 12, 2012 at the age of 62 years in Kamloops, British Columbia, Canada. She was an accomplished beader and knowledgeable in the medicine wheel teaching. She is interred in the Bonaparte Cemetery, Bonaparte Indian Reserve, Cache Creek, Canada.

[58] A Room With A Pew, www.roomwithapew, July 7, 2014.

[59] "It is likely that Marie Dorion and Sacajawea knew one another. Peter Stark notes the similarities between the two women in his book *Astoria*: both women were originally based in the then small settlement of St. Louis, and they were both wives of interpreters in the burgeoning Missouri fur trade." Wikipedia, 2014.

*

About The Author

Sharon Doubiago's memoir, *My Father's Love: Portrait of the Poet as a Young Woman,* Volume 1 (Wild Ocean Press, 2009), was a finalist in the Northern California Book Awards in Creative Nonfiction, 2010. *My Father's Love: Portrait of the Poet as a Woman*, Volume 2, was published in 2011 (Wild Ocean Press). *Love on the Streets: Selected and New Poems* (University of Pittsburgh Press, 2008) received the Glenna Luschei Distinguished Poet Award and was a finalist in the Paterson New Jersey Poetry Prize. She has written two dozen books of poetry and prose, most notably the epic poem *Hard Country* (West End Press, 1982; 1999), *Psyche Drives The Coast* (Empty Bowl Press, 1990) for which she holds the Oregon Book Award for Poetry, the book-length poem *South America Mi Hija* (University of Pittsburgh Press, 1992), which was nominated twice for the National Book Award, and the story collections *El Niño* (Lost Roads Press, 1989) and *The Book of Seeing With One's Own Eyes* (Graywolf Press, 1988), which was selected to the Oregon Culture Heritage list: *Literary Oregon, 100 Books, 1800-2000.* She holds three Pushcart Prizes for poetry and fiction, two Oregon Institute of Literary Art Fellowships, and a California Arts Council Award. She's published over a hundred essays—from the personal and creative, to the scholarly. Her new collection of memoir stories, *Why She Loved Him,* is circulating, as is her latest poetry collection, *Naked To The Earth.* She is a board member of PEN Oakland.